P is for Prostitution

Other titles by Charlotte Rodgers

The Bloody Sacrifice: A Personal Experience of Contemporary Blood Rites

A Contemporary Western Book Of The Dead (edited Lydia Maskell)

Other Titles by Ruth Ramsden

Radical Desire: Kink & Magical Sex (With Mark Ramsden)

Blue Murder at the Pink Parrot

P is for Prostitution

An A-Z of a harsh life survived

Charlotte Rodgers

(Illustrated by Ruth Ramsden)

First paperback Edition
2nd impression

ublished by
andrake of Oxford
O Box 250
XFORD
X1 1AP (UK)

CIP catalogue record for this book is available from the British ibrary and the US Library of Congress.

'The way to despair is to refuse to have any kind of experience...'

Flannery O'Connor

Daddy was an exclamation mark, exploding on blank walls,
I was a biblioteque hero, supporting Atlas' balls,
Roller skating on Freudian slips,
Pussy footing through the fly leafings
Of fellow social misfits.
Well read, intellectually fed neurosis,
Genetically perfected psychosis
Penis Envy
Poison Ivy
Piss and Raving.
Something in the woodshed gave you a fright,
Rumplestiltskin will tell you anytime
Its prick is worse than its bite.
Go-go virgins in discotheque cages
Venus in politically unsound furs
Lectures on the latest psychoanalytical magus
Romulus Remus Oedipus
Sucking dugs like common curs.
Psychoanalyse, disembowel and theorise,
Penis Envy Poison Ivy
Something in the woodshed gave you a fright,
Rumplestiltskin will tell you anytime,
Its prick is worse than its bite.

C. Rodgers 1985

Contents

Foreword

'**P is for Prostitution**' is a personal memoir, which explores episodes and experiences from Charlotte Rodgers' difficult chaotic life, through her childhood and into early adulthood. At times this book made me feel incredibly sad and much of it was alien to my own comfortable, relatively trouble-free youth. However, her story captivated me and I found myself wanting to find out more about the girl being described. Also, as a woman who grew up during the same decades, I recognized the underlying misogyny of the era and the rules that women were expected to observe. Both Charlotte and her mother suffered in different ways because they were unable to live within narrow definitions of womanhood.

The Primer structure works particularly well and gives the impression of bringing order to a fragmented and chaotic existence. It comments on the nature of individual memory that is not linear and makes connections between disparate incidents and episodes. This form enables the reader to think for herself and reflect on how Charlotte's childhood and formative experiences affect her situation as she grows up.

Throughout *P is for Prostitution*, despite the chaos of a life dominated by addictions and illnesses, Charlotte remains a creative and intellectually curious person. Her attraction to similar damaged anarchic souls both as friends and lovers can be seen at various points in her book. Near the end she refers to 'the person from Porlock', a debt collector who interrupted Coleridge whilst he was writing Kubla Khan. Charlotte writes, "I feel as if I too had a debt collector knocking on the door of my life, and breaking and permanently redirecting my concentration." The book conveys a real sense that Charlotte's creativity and intellect was somehow misdirected at a young age towards a nihilistic and savage existence. It also traces the constant, durable thread of spirituality in her life. This is fascinating given her early encounters with Catholicism.

The book powerfully communicates the devastating effect of physical and mental abuse on Charlotte's whole family. The suffering her parents endured as children impacts on Charlotte's life and leads to a lack of stability and security when she is growing up. Charlotte too is terrorized as a child whilst under the 'care' of her Grandmother. The sexual repression, religious fanaticism and cruelty that lie behind this abuse are horrifying. Children's lack of power and the lasting consequences of adult neglect and brutality are recurrent themes.

The reader is able to observe how Charlotte's eating disorders are caused by a desire to gain some control and how the perception that thinness equals happiness and acceptance actually appears to have almost the opposite effect. This is something that all women can relate to at some level. The book also gave me an insight into addiction and the kind of existence that inevitably goes with it. Her experiences are distinctive but they do reflect the times she lived in and the alternative lifestyle that seemed to be offered by the world of drugs and music. The attraction of losing control and finding a different reality is explored. However, the destructive power of addiction ultimately makes life unbearable.

Charlotte's discussion of sex in *P is for Prostitution* is thought-provoking and brave. Her unconventional attitudes and approach made me think hard about the way women are condemned and vilified for sexual transgressions. Moreover, it made me consider how women and children are so often the victims of abuse and the hypocrisy that existed about this when we were growing up and still does to a large extent. Women who transgressed the sexual norms or accepted codes of behaviour were seen as to blame for the abuse they suffered, rather than as victims.

Fundamentally, this is a fascinating articulate and engrossing book. It describes experiences and feelings with which many people, especially women, will identify. I think people will enjoy Charlotte's honesty and will want to read on and find out how she manages to get through and eventually change her life permanently. Charlotte takes you into divergent worlds, often frighteningly disordered; but the creative, compassionate and intelligent woman that she is today, is always there despite the destructive forces in her early life.

Jane Hunt

Acknowledgments

To the Gods and the humans who have always loved me.

Huge thanks to the wonderful Ruth Ramsden who channelled my past into such apt imagery, helping me rein the chaos into tidy structures

My gratitude also goes to Jane Hunt who coped so well with her long term friend's newly revealed history AND was willing to read and constructively comment on it.

Acknowledgement also to Mogg and Kim Morgan who have never let me down, and my dear sister who was so frightened about the ghosts the writing of this might bring back to haunt me.

Most of all, I thank the dead who have never ceased to be there for me; may they continue to have an incredibly lavish and perpetually fun party.

Vowels, Consonants and Other Building Blocks: An Introduction

Several years of exploring and writing about death and cults of the ancestors have led to my putting this, more personal book together.

As I looked at how necessary acknowledgement of the past can be to solidify the sense of self, both as an individual and a member of a community; flashes of my own, personal history came back to me.

I started to re connect with this and found a catalogue of youthful dead and missing loved ones. This was no surprise to me given the way that we lived our lives at that time, but was no less saddening.

Whilst the people concerned were not blood relatives, they were part of who I was at that time. They were very much my family of choice in our shared inability or refusal to accept the terms that mainstream existence at that time offered.

I decided to reclaim this time and a lost part of myself, by going back and recording some of my rather erratic recollections.

Initially I was worried that writing this could be self-indulgence or an exercise in personal exploration and poor man's psychoanalysis that shouldn't be put out to a wider audience.

However the times and places I lived in, and the way I experienced them, hold things which I believe are core to many who struggle to find their place in this strange world.

Putting such a chaotic mass of events into order could have proved an impossibility until it became apparent to me that my early years were very much about finding a set of rules to live by, thus the original subtitle, 'A Modern Primer'.

Using the alphabet to give order to these memories was a continuation of the primer concept and works well for me. My life was not lived in a straight line and my rather scrappy memory would have rebelled against too linear a form of organisation.

The time span this book encompasses is the 1970s to the 1990s and the backdrop moves between Hong Kong, Australia, London and New Zealand.

This was a time when digital watches were rare and expensive things; China was hard line communist and undeveloped; the Internet was unheard of and there was still a wall dividing Berlin. Graphic novels were on the ascent; only the super-rich had credit cards, and AIDS was just a whisper that could kill in its utterance.

When I was diagnosed with bulimia it was a relatively unknown condition that the medical establishment were unsure how to approach.

I cleaned up as crack was just starting to make its presence known and I was already seeing changes it had made in the junkie community.

Drug using rapidly became even more associated with violence, users burned out much more quickly, if they survived.

When I stopped using drugs I was 30 and considered relatively young in the 'recovery' community, but 18 years later I see women burned out by the time they are 15 or 16.

I was one of the first waves of people to go into drug and alcohol rehab, and sad to say the women's only treatment centre I was in, due to lack of funding, no longer exists.

However the core of the experiences in this book isn't era specific but is more about one individual's rather rocky road through her early years.

One thing that I feel I should add.

Readers may find my tone to be detached and even perceive a certain lack of emotion.

I was and still am an internalised person, something that may have led to some of my problems over the years.

I look at old photographs of myself and I see a lovely looking girl who seemed locked in her own world.

Eventually I couldn't stay in that private place anymore, despite ever increasing amounts of emotion suppressing drugs. When I left rehab I had a graduation of sorts, a ceremony where I was presented with a butterfly brooch. As I was given my pin, Sister Rosemary who ran the home said that when I arrived at the facility I was like the survivor of a serious car crash; locked in trauma.

Walking away from my car crash life, with its explorations, adventures, and ever increasing horror was when I really started to live.

It was a very different world then, but in many respects, the way we all live and develop has not changed at all.

A is for Aeroplane

I was unusual for someone of my generation in New Zealand, in my frequent travel by aeroplane.

Most people of that era travelled around New Zealand by car, as flying was prohibitively expensive. However my family in their frequent migrations were always in a hurry. They generally had their travel costs covered by whatever company my father was working for, and never owned a car (probably a good thing as I suspect both my parents would have been a serious liability behind the wheel), so flying was the only real option.

My first solo flight was when I was five or so and I enjoyed being the centre of attention of passengers and the air hostess who plied me with huge quantities of the sweets they used to distribute on planes to stop your ears popping.

When I was in my teens I generally caught the ferry between the North and South Island but on one occasion my friends and I flew on a six seater Air Albatross flight, an airline which only operated four years before it folded due to its dismal record of plane crashes and disappearances. First we had a massive hit of speed in the airport toilets then rushed to the aeroplane for take-off, and with each consequent dramatic drop of the plane over the choppy waters of the Cook Strait, the rush from the speed would return. At one point we hurtled down after hitting an air pocket and were so close to the heaving waters, we would have been able to lean out of the plane and touch the waves; although a tiny portion of our amphetamine addled brains was still functioning enough to indicate that this wasn't a safe and sensible option. A runway was being bulldozed clear as we landed, which added to the excitement.

When I was sixteen I started taking long haul flights to visit my family in Hong Kong. At that time planes, the smoking section anyway, were hard-core partying zones. I was generally exceptionally dilapidated by the time I disembarked. My family would lay bets as to whether I emerge from the arrivals gate bloated (drink) or emaciated (drugs) and what colour my hair would be.

These bets enlarged to whether I would actually arrive, when on one occasion my luggage safely emerged from the plane without me, as I was still drinking in the transit lounge bar in Sydney and had missed my connecting flight.

I experienced the joys of Air Lanka planes (a wing catching fire) Air China (cardboard lunchboxes and flights that the airlines pretended never existed rather than admit they had been lost or crashed) meeting long lost friends in tiny airports in Papua New Guinea, and near death experiences on tiny propeller planes.

Somehow I never managed to join the much lauded 'mile high club'. Although I enjoyed many a fumble in airport bars and transit lounges, by the time I actually boarded a plane I was generally so trashed and dishevelled I was more enthusiastic about the free food and alcohol, than a quick congress with a stranger in an enclosed space.

B is for : Bulimia

B is for Bulimia

I had always been a solid child, with a body that appeared older than its actual years. I think this was partially due to genes and partially to a personality that preferred to daydream and read rather than to exercise and play with other children. At age eleven I was large chested, had reached my full height, was already menstruating and had moved beyond solid to obese.

This worried my mother who had major size issues of her own (as did my father but at this point he had already gone AWOL). She took me to the doctor where I was weighed and found to be 72kg, which was massively overweight for a child of my age.

I went home with my mother where my friend Maria was waiting for me with a large bar of expensive chocolate. I shared the chocolate with my friend, but as I had decided to start serious dieting, I vomited after eating it and then firmly integrated bulimia into my dieting strategy.

I lost a few pounds but remained bulimic and by age 14 I decided to kill myself through starvation by way of protest at how powerless I felt in such an alien world.

In retrospect I can see that this was a high drama teenage angst indulgence, but this doesn't nullify how much pain I was actually in at the time.

Sadly as I became slimmer, the boys that had previously mocked me found me attractive which made me more disillusioned and unhappy.

My weight loss accelerated, and as is detailed later in this primer, I was briefly hospitalised. For years I fluctuated in size and staggered between severe bulimia and anorexia. Opiate use controlled it to an extent, but for many years my life was dictated by my food intake and having convenient places to throw up.

When I was 25 I had new front teeth fitted as the constant vomiting had eroded my own. Shortly afterwards I went to Yangzhou in China, where I was sitting by the Yangtze River thinking, 'I'm bored, I don't want this anymore', so I let go of the compulsion.

I eventually figured out that I threw up instead of getting angry, so I had to learn how to get angry. An overnight revelation that took much longer in its implementing; my eating disorder still affects my life, but no longer rules it.

C is for: Christmas

C is for Christmas (Duck and Dinner)

Early 1990s and without money as usual, but with a surplus of drugs due to Martyn's latest robbery of a chemist shop. I felt inspired to go hunting for something special for Christmas dinner.

At the end of the long street on which I lived was a park with a duck pond, so I spent Christmas Eve creating a solution of Valium and Notec aka Mickey Finn, in which I soaked a stale half loaf of bread. I stayed up all night, fuelling myself for the task ahead with the necessary inebriants. Daybreak saw me at the edge of the pond feeding the ducks with the drug laced bread, a machete at my side.

Now there were enough sedatives in that bread to wipe out the audience of a small concert venue but the ducks didn't react in the manner I had hoped. For a start they stayed, in tight formation at the other side of the pond where I couldn't swipe them with my blade. Well I actually could and did swipe, but it didn't achieve anything except hostile noises and stares from the ducks.

The occasional bird that did move out of the group was quickly warned by the frenetic quacking of its peers, to return to the fold.

Whilst these sinister actions were unusual I didn't notice any other behavioural changes in the creatures, although I did see a duck do a somersault before it raced to join its kin at their safe vantage point.

However the Gods still loved me and as I was walking home, despondent, I found a duck that was freshly killed by a car so we were still able to have our special Christmas dinner, duck with apricot, as we had no oranges.

C is for Commitment

Commitment has never been my strong point, be it to a person, lifestyle or abode.

Whilst my spiritual and political beliefs have always been relatively constant, the mainstays of my existence have tended to reflect my desire for stimulus and change, rather than stability. Needless to say these attitudes have not created committed long-term relationships in my life.

Once I became consciously sexually active, I embarked upon a long series of 'encounters' rather than relationships. I tended not to take things very seriously and was always bemused when someone I had sex with assumed that it was the start of a relationship.

I had a few great loves all of which ended badly, generally due to my drinking, drug use and tendency to sleep with whoever I wanted rather than adhere to mainstream standards of monogamy.

One of my longest partnerships was with a musician, Martyn, in New Zealand. Martyn was the founder member of a cult band, had an opiate habit, and was incredibly intelligent.

I was living with a friend, Hazel after sleeping with a few of the wrong people again. This had effectively rendered me homeless until Hazel rescued me and gave me a room in her house.

I was involved in a few flirtations with potential. Martyn used to regularly pop around to visit Hazel, and then spend some time chatting with me.

I liked talking to him, as our respective creative intelligences were highly compatible, although I didn't initially feel sexually attracted. Martyn started to visit me daily, each time bringing a drug related gift.

All these generally opiate based presents were much appreciated as they also stopped me drinking. This was a great thing as when I drank I invariable blacked out and often did something disturbing.

One day Martyn didn't come to visit. I started to withdraw so this time I went to visit him realising that I had developed a drug habit.

In some ways my time with Martyn was wonderful. He was the first person to court me. I loved his mind; we had great sex and creatively were dynamite together.

He genuinely appreciated my intellect and the art I produced, which meant a lot to me in my youthful insecurity, however the drugs proved a problem.

Martyn had deliberately given me drugs as he thought that I was better off using opiates rather than drinking; he was a very loud and political advocate of the decriminalisation of opiates and their ability to cure everything from ME to Candida.

Martyn set me up with his own doctor so I was able to get a script for tinc.camph.opii ...very de Quincy.

However despite the prescription opiates Martyn still felt the need for extra drugs. There was the constant bartering between us and other addicts; he would occasionally burgle a chemist shop or local medical school for more of something; barbiturates being a particular favourite.

Okay we had the artistic credentials, but still lived in an addict's world with all the things which that bought with it on a financial, legal, emotional and physical level. Members of our group would die or kill themselves; I was emaciated with few injectable veins left. My morning hit would often see me ill with withdrawal symptoms whilst someone tried to insert a needle in my hand, foot, groin, or as a last resort, a vein in my neck.

I tried to come off opiates, but whilst living in that environment it proved to be impossible; so I left Martyn and New Zealand to try and build a semblance of a life.

My next long-term relationship was some years later, in London. I was working as a trainee pub manager in a pub in Brixton, and yes I had a habit again, although this time around I strictly delineated my junkie life and mundane life, with no-one in the pub I worked and later lived knowing about my addiction.

Geoff was also a trainee pub manager. We eventually had sex, which was so amazing that when he proposed in a post coital flush, I accepted. Geoff was very much a South London boy; a nice man but not my kind at all. He liked to drink and fight, to eat curries and go on trips to Spain with groups of his peers, where they behaved in the traditional way that causes documentaries to be made about the lager lout British tourist.

We really had nothing in common but I was 25 years old and desperate to be saved. Eventually I told him about my addiction, something which was completely beyond his realm of comprehension. He accompanied me to London's Maudsley Hospital where I was put on methadone and informed that I had Hep C which would eventually kill me! At that time Hep C was a new discovery and the medical powers that be were very negative about its long term effects.

I was pregnant when we married in the less than salubrious Peckham Rye registry office. I had been recommended to stay on methadone as the trauma of withdrawal could have caused even more problems during my very difficult pregnancy, but this didn't prevent an eventual still birth. When I lost the child, the marriage was damaged irreparably and we moved to Geoff's family home in Dartford where things degenerated further.

Dartford was the most alien environment I, in all my travels, have ever come across. We lived in Temple Hill Housing Estate where I worked in a pub whilst Geoff became a deliveryman for appliances. I was incredibly lonely and alienated, relying on visits to junkie friends in London to create a semblance of happiness in my life.

We had a Staffordshire bull terrier that we had been given as a wedding present that Geoff called Chelsea. She was my main source of company in the days, as I often worked night shifts. I would start my day with methadone and Prozac. If I had been to London recently I would lock Chelsea out of the bedroom whilst I had a hit of Heroin. Later in the day I would start drinking, and would generally take some speed as well so the drink wouldn't affect my ability to work.

I'd come home in the evenings and Geoff would be in his bathrobe watching television and drinking, so I would have a drink with him and sometimes a joint. Often I would pass out on the floor and wake up to him kicking me awake; not horribly hard, just enough to make me realise I was worth nothing.

Finally I left Geoff. I was homeless for a time before I moved in with a speed dealer.

I was admitted into a series of treatment centres. Geoff never visited me, although I rang him once to apologise for my behaviour. I divorced him sight unseen some years later. Like much of my past Geoff became just a disquieting memory.

D is for Dry Ice

Like most teenagers I was very enthusiastic about having parties, and whilst living in Wellington, New Zealand and having inordinate amounts of money due to my work in brothels, I was better suited than most people of my own age to put on spectacular, highly indulgent productions.

My 18th birthday celebrations started early with some bad speed to help my organisation of the event get properly underway. By the time the party started the dry ice and dry ice machine that was one of my presents had created several feet of impenetrable fog hanging over the floor. I was incredibly wasted. My friend, Jane, lying next to me, complaining about her sudden blindness. I sat next to her, paralysed, trying to avoid sliding under the dry ice miasma where many unconscious bodies lay.

Some time before we had a new neighbour move next door, from Australia. He was one of the first in Sydney to be diagnosed as HIV positive. The very public and hysterical announcements in the media about his condition had made his life hell, so he moved to Wellington.

At one point I heard Jane yelp, there is someone with AIDS in this room. The room cleared (of those who were conscious anyway) only my new neighbour and I remained. Shortly afterwards he hung himself.

D is for Dwarf (named Pedro)

I spent the millennium in Indonesia with a lover. We decided to go to a deserted beach on the far side of Bali to see in the new century but somehow managed to end up in a rundown, rubbish strewn area in a room infested with bedbugs and fleas.

The beachfront had a small bar filled with old German hippies who had come to Bali in the 1960s but never left. Pedro, a dwarf with painted green fingernails was distributing magic mushrooms. There was a rather seedy and Bosch-like feel to the proceedings. Midnight of the new century saw my lover and me in our room, wrapped in mosquito nets and coated in tea tree oil as an insect repellent, trying to sleep it all away.

E is for Escape

Escaping was the proverbial raison d'être for most of my life. The methods I used were primitive and less than ingenious, generally producing a new form of entrapment rather than freedom. In my earlier years with Martyn I would clumsily try to end my relationship with him by having ostentatious affairs.

At one point I fled to a friend's family home while his parents were on a long trip in Europe. I took my new lover, Pockets, with me. Martyn would visit every day bringing drugs for me (so that I wouldn't withdraw) and for Pockets (to be sociable and polite).

Whether it was truth or urban myth, Pockets had acquired his moniker by running a school for pickpockets in Aro Street, Wellington. He had been in the Merchant Navy and had the required rolling, sailor's walk. He was tough and very macho; not my usual type at all.

Pockets had scars on his penis from various primitive treatments for VD. I think he referred to one of these methods as the 'umbrella treatment', which entailed a long metal apparatus that opened out after it had been inserted into the urethra, scraping it clean as it was removed. Rather than being repelled, I found it fascinating, which perhaps says a lot about the way my mind worked.

He was a good friend and great fun. In my brief time with him we partied hard, consumed large amounts of drugs, and had fantastic sex.

I eventually returned to Martyn, and the large drug bill he had run up to get me back. Pockets died some years later of a cerebral haemorrhage.

F is for Father

Writing about my father will be like writing about a Chinese whisper that somehow inseminated your mother.

Andrew, my father was born in Edinburgh and hailed from a Catholic Scottish mining family that several generations before, had emigrated from Ireland. When the Second World War started my paternal grandfather left his usual job planting explosives to break up a coal seam, to fight. The moment he was gone, my grandmother abandoned her many children, and fled.

I never was really able to ascertain how many children she had had before she left. I think she had eleven pregnancies by the time she was 30, some of which were miscarriages; a few died very young. The remainder, which included my father, tried to survive by themselves after their mother left, but eventually their parentless state was discovered. They were separated to be brought up in respective nun and brother run schools.

My father looked to have a glass eye but it was actually washed out and discoloured due to a blow by a priest. He also had an intriguing hole the size of a fifty pence piece, covered in fine skin, on his calf. This had been the result of another beating by a priest, which created an infection in the bone that had required surgery.

He had a great aptitude for drawing, and had been offered a scholarship to art school. But men of that era didn't do such things, so he left school at eleven to work in the mines. As soon as legally possible, he joined the Merchant Navy.

Andrew was a self-educated, bright, creative, very masculine man who loved drinking and gambling. He was extremely fit (five feet five inches and eleven stone, he never allowed that weight to change) and very charismatic.

The ship he was working on was docked in Wellington, when he met my beautiful, damaged mother. They fell madly, destructively in love; I was conceived and they married.

On their wedding night my father stayed up all night playing cards with staff at the hotel where they were honeymooning. He lost all his and my mother's money, their wedding rings and their watches.

My father was very tidy and very controlled. He trained himself as a chef, at which he excelled.

Our family household finances were invariably in a state of feast or famine according to his success or failure at the races or cards. He would regularly abandon my mother, once disappearing for over a year (his return resulted in my sister's conception). I was brought up in the midst of this sad relationship that illustrated how love can erode and degrade.

The times I saw him mid work binge I would occasionally accompany him to the races, or sometimes a film but more often visit him in the kitchens of restaurants and hotels he worked.

At times my father would drift into a deep depression. He wouldn't work and instead lay in bed in a dark room for months with his hands bandaged after violent bouts of compulsive hand washing.

My mother would be drugged, weeping and often naked. Sometimes they would fight and Andrew would hurl teapots at her, leaving me an abiding memory of teapots hitting walls, tea trickling down and staining them.

Near the end of the relationship my mother, hit him on the head when he was sleeping and broke many of the small bones in her hand. She left my father when I was ten years old. Andrew moved to Sydney in Australia where he had a course of electro convulsive therapy for his compulsive obsessive disorder. After discharging himself from hospital he was never heard from again.

I still have a copy of the last letter he sent my mother, saying that he was putting up post-it notes containing essential information around his flat, as after ECT one often had memory lapses.

He also talked of looking forward to his first orgasm after treatment as in *One Flew over the Cuckoo's Nest* it was said that post shock treatment sex would pay out like a slot machine, in silver dollars.

F is for Feral (children)

I suppose it is inevitable that in my meanderings through the counter culture in different eras and countries, I would encounter disturbed and damaged children, as well as balanced and well adjusted ones.

I came across one of my more memorable examples of feral children when I was living in London in the 1990s. 'Big John', his wife Sarah, and John's two younger brothers were from Glasgow. They made their living from co-ordinated raids on supermarkets. They would steal batteries, razors, cigarettes and alcohol, which were untraceable and easy to shift quickly, for an excellent profit.

They were all addicted to heroin and crack and moved to London when they were blacklisted from all shops and supermarkets in Glasgow, and the police had them under constant and intense scrutiny. I met them through some junkie friends, who would occasionally score from the same dealer.

Sarah had two children and was pregnant when I first met her, although she was still using drugs. We talked a bit and I found out that she and John had initially been neighbours married to other people in an old style tenement estate in Glasgow. They had fallen deeply in love and left their respective partners to live together, which is when they started using A class drugs. This all happened when they were very young. They were actually nice, although frighteningly hard.

I occasionally went around to the squat in Tulse Hill Estate they were all living in, to wait for Big John and his crew to return after selling stolen goods and scoring. In some ways their relationship was very traditional. Sarah would never participate in the burglaries, only the men.

The flat had a mattress on the floor that was covered in rubbish and human waste. Their two children, one of four the other about seven, were naked and could not talk. However they loved their children, were looking forward to the next one being born. There was an incredible loyalty among these people. They were all caught after one burglary but Big John's younger brother took the blame and was imprisoned so the family head could stay free to look after and provide for the others.

G is for Grandmother (on my mother's side, otherwise known as 'Nana')

As with my mother in the 'pills' section, I could lead this entry with, 'she was very much a woman of her time'. However dumping responsibilities of one's actions on the morality of the era is a cop out and a less than cunning form of evasion.

My grandmother was an intelligent woman of whom I know very little, as that generation didn't talk of themselves or their past. My mother rarely alluded to her parents' lives or her own childhood, although they were the source of a black hole of neurosis in our lives.

My great-grandfather married three times; putting his first wife in an institution when she proved unable to have children; wearing the second one down to a youthful death through repeated pregnancies and overwork, then moving onto his final wife who was a tiny cowed figure who managed to survive his bullying.

One story that perhaps gives a key to his personality was that he promised my grandmother Isa, as a child, a pony if she was good. She was exceptionally well behaved and her father would tell her that she was doing well and she would get her pony soon. After nearly a year and a half he told her that she would get her reward the next day. That day came and he told her that she was an, 'April Fool!'

In her late teens Isa became a nun, but left before taking her final vows, although she kept a strong streak of Roman Catholic religiosity which intensified to mania as she became older.

She had wanted to become a doctor but her father considered that to be too masculine a profession so she became a nurse at which she excelled. She married late in life and adopted my mother as it was a "moral thing to do".

She physically and mentally abused my mother then did the same to me when I stayed there during times of more than usual family instability, although to a much lesser degree.

Living with her was living with fear and religion in its darkest manifestation.

The strapping; the hard smacking on the legs and arms; the pinching and hair pulling; the bleeding when hair pins were rammed into my head during the crafting of three face pulling plaits to create a freakish appearance that caused jeers when I went to school; all were nothing compared to the days of waiting for punishment for unknown transgressions.

My grandfather was a large earthy man, who kept himself to himself letting my grandmother do what she wanted.

They slept in separate beds as she found his New Zealand 'bloke' crudeness with its loud celebration of bodily functions, an offence. Granddad would push his false teeth out, pick his nose, pull out a pen knife at the dinner table to peel his fruit (ignoring the linen napkin and side plate) and would utter obscure rhythmic gems such as, 'strike me pink woman, strike me pink' or 'if a man saw a man in man's beans, would a man tell a man what a man means, in a man's beans'.

In retrospect I would say that his behaviour was contrived or exaggerated to enrage my grandmother. He was actually a gentle, well-educated man, who wore a custom made, built up shoe and relied on a stick to walk.

When he was in his late teens he slipped while loading hay into a baler. His leg was dragged into the rollers up to his knee and crushed, although he was rescued before the blades did more than slice the end off his boots. He spent a long time convalescing during which time he did the most exquisite needle point which was a type of therapy then for men with severe injuries. It was incredible that he didn't have his leg amputated, although it never fully healed. I still remember him regularly dressing his leg with bandages after applying some evil smelling, thick pink ointment.

Nana died of a brain cancer. Staying with her whilst the dementia caused rapid mental deterioration was the only time the house wasn't full of dark shadows. I was only ten and found Nana's shift from fastidious cleanliness to obvious lack of hygiene strange, but oddly empowering.

My grandmother had been a diet controlled diabetic for years, and food had always been plain, horrible and to be finished even if it meant sitting at the table for many, many hours. Now I had become cook and my limited repertoire provided quantities of scones and pancakes with cream and jam, with my grandfather filling in the gaps by making frequent visits to the fish and chip shop.

The day no longer revolved around prayers and church. I didn't need to pull the black-out blinds in my bedroom at night. The terrifying image over my bed of Christ writhing on the cross would no longer come for me once the darkness fell.

My grandmother's mental decline was obvious but the local Church happily took the increasingly large donations she made before she was finally hospitalised. I cannot remember a funeral, and don't even know where she is buried but I believe that her religion created hell for her, just as she created hell in this world for the children with whom she was entrusted.

H is for Hitchhiking

Hitchhiking was my transportation of choice for many years. Aside from the money saved, it also brought many adventures which provided an interesting edge to the experience.

Whilst I was in my early teens, I and a favoured few friends used to drink copiously, take a cocktail of pills stolen from my mother, and hitchhike to parties around Wellington (although we occasionally ended up further afield, once on the inter island ferry drinking in the crew's bar) which generally meant that we ended up in sick bay en masse on a Monday morning, trying between us to piece together a recollection of the weekends activities.

At 14 I hitchhiked with my 12 year old sister to Dunedin to visit a boyfriend of mine. On our way back to Wellington we were given a lift by several rodeo cowboys returning home with their empty horsebox at the end of a tour. Initially open and generous they were drinking heavily and gradually becoming more lascivious. It peaked when they parked in a desolate paddock at the base of Mount Manganui. My sister's crying that she was only 12 didn't deter them. We eventually managed to lock them out of the car, and they passed out in the horse box.

Early the next morning, whilst the cowboys slept, we crossed the fields to the main road. We walked until we were given a lift by the only passing car, a mail truck.

My sister never hitchhiked again but I continued for many years.

Sometimes I would have a fantastic time; meeting people to party with, being given a bucket full of marijuana from a man who had just harvested his crop of grass, or being fed and given money to stay in hotels rather than having to sleep at the side of a road overnight.

There were also, of course, the horrible incidents. On one occasion I had sex for $50 rather than risk rape. On another I was forced at knife point to give someone a blow job at the end of which I was pushed out of the car at night into an immense space of nothing between Dunedin and Christchurch. In the first case I was able to cope pretty well; perhaps the money made it seem less abusive.

The second incident was terrifying. I had known near the moment I got into the car that something was wrong; quickly realising I was in a dangerous situation. I tried to get the driver to stop the car and let me out. When he did pull over he became aggressive, produced a knife and wanted to have sex. I told him I had herpes, which prompted a lot of verbal and physical abuse. He forced me perform oral sex on him. He then started the car and as he was slowly coming off the verge, onto the road, he leaned over, opened the door and shoved me out.

After he pulled away I went into the dislocated space I used to go into when something traumatic happened. I disconnected from my body and became very confused. I ran from one side of the road to other trying to flag down a car to go... anywhere... until I got a lift from an off duty policeman going back to Christchurch.

I stayed with friends for several days before I was loaned money to get a bus back home to Dunedin. The policeman encouraged me to press charges but what was the point? A drug addicted, occasional prostitute who was hitchhiking alone, charging someone for sexual assault; not a hope.

Much later I hitchhiked through Europe with a friend, travelling through Germany when it was still divided. On the borders of Berlin there was a turnover of hundreds of hitchhikers per hour as hitching was a common form of transport then.

Within a few years, however, I stopped travelling like this. Active addiction created stagnation and a dislike of venturing far from my home base. As fear of withdrawal grew stronger so also did my fear of being too far from my suppliers.

It is ironic really; it was drug using that prompted my hitchhiking, saving money to spend on drugs that perpetuated it, and drugs rather than bad experiences that stopped me doing it.

H is for : Hotel

H is for Hotels (and Motels)

My father was a chef for a company called Dominion Breweries. This combined with his intolerance for sameness and being in one place for any extended (anything over six months) period of time, meant that we often were residents in a variety of hotels, motels and boarding houses.

On reflection we very much lived with a refugee mentality; superfluous possessions were not an option, a suitcase per person was the maximum allowed and we needed to always be prepared to 'go'.

When our minor hoard descended on a new home we had to re-equip ourselves with household equipment courtesy of Woolworths. There was not much emphasis on kitchen implements as my mother didn't cook and was loath to have food in the house (one ate it, and therefore got fat) so we ate in the places my father worked.

These places often had interesting characters.

There was Carmelita, the 90 year old bedridden Spanish woman who lived with her lover and carer, Pat. She had been a flamenco dancer, and was immortalised in a huge painting of herself in her prime, dancing in full regalia, hanging in her bedroom. She would often lift her long white nightgown to show us how wonderful her legs still were (and they were).

We would troop downstairs to her room for an afternoon tea of lemonade and cake served by Pat, with Carmelita holding court from her bed.

In Nelson there was another Pat who actually looked very similar to Carmelita's beau, except that this was a woman, albeit one who dressed as a man. I suspect that this Pat, like my father, was a gambler. I would on occasion see them huddled together comparing form and racing slips.

Another motel we briefly lived in was in Christchurch. This place was 1970s modern. It was supposedly temporary until the restaurant my father was working found us more permanent accommodation.

I used to play with Charlene, the owner's daughter, in the grounds behind the building, digging bunkers in the dirt and generally messing around.

There was an older man who also lived on the premises that took an interest in Charlene and myself and with a child's intuition we knew that he wanted something from us and could be counted on to buy us sweets. Somehow I ended up alone with him in his house. I must have been seven or so. Something of a rather basic sexual nature occurred. I was giggling with my sister about this a short time later. My mother heard and by the time my father came home the proverbial shit had hit the fan and I was being interviewed by police. However as my mother had already told Charlene's father and he had aggressively confronted our neighbour, who very quickly departed; the police had little they could do.

I was able to milk the incident for some time, saying that I was frightened that the abuser would come back So my father met me after school and walked me home.

After a while all these places became a blur, as did most of those years until my father left and the family became relatively settled.

One particular hotel room, which I remember, was when I was 17. I had left the hospital where the attempt had been made to treat my bulimia and had been attending an eating disorders support group. A researcher for a documentary on eating disorders for New Zealand television contacted me through the group and I was filmed talking through experiences of the illness.

Meanwhile I was losing weight rapidly and having frequent fits due to a severe electrolyte imbalance. I was also taking a lot of drugs, some of them intravenously.

My family had left New Zealand at this point so a family friend, Ross, decided to help me out. He drove me up to Rotarua, booked me into a hotel there for a week, leaving me food, a return bus ticket and space to try and clear my head.

That night after a series of huge binge and vomiting sessions I consumed my week's supply of food. I was lying on the motel's single bed, watching television when the documentary came on. I still remember moving in and out of fits, see images of me on the screen drifting in and out of consciousness saying, 'but I'm all right now'.

I changed my bus ticket and went back to Wellington immediately, moved out of my flat in Carrington Street and tried to start again.

Whilst I didn't succeed in finding stability at that point, I believe the move prolonged my life for quite a few years.

H is for Hospital

Oh this will be a long section! My first long stint in a psychiatric hospital was when I was 16 for treatment of anorexia and bulimia. Although I was very underweight, the hospital was initially more concerned about the fits I was having due to a dangerously low electrolyte level.

The decision to section me was a last minute one. I had been monitored for some time in our weekly family counselling sessions, which were followed by a medical examination that included blood tests and weighing.

That particular week the post family counselling session check up revealed my weight had dropped below the agreed upon danger point (42 kg). I was admitted immediately.

Initially I was more upset about having to cancel a hitchhiking trip to Dunedin to visit a boyfriend. I didn't realise the ramifications of a hospital stay. In those days treatment for anorexia and the then little known bulimia, was 'Behavioural Modification; Reward-Punishment Treatment'.

I was interviewed by three doctors with a hidden audience behind a two way mirror. I was quizzed about my eating and drinking habits, as well as menstruation and my sex life.

My clothes were taken away. I was given a backless hospital gown and was put on complete bed rest. The regime was focused around food and weight gain. Counselling and therapy wasn't to be included in the regime until much later. I was allowed no radio, books or television. If I behaved I would gradually be able to earn these privileges.

I was accompanied to the toilet, supervised in my many (very large meals) with high cal drinks in between. I was drugged when I proved to be a difficult and verbose patient.

Initially I was allowed visitors. I had a constant stream of well wishers. One boyfriend (I had a few) coming to visit me on a unicycle bearing hash brownies to stimulate my appetite. Another brought 'cheer up' themed mix tapes.

Whilst I was still allowed that freedom of movement I wandered around the ward, and met several of the other patients. Jenny was classically anorexic, had tried to cut her wrists and had near severed her hand. Surgeons managed to reattach it but most movement and sensation was lost.

We became friends. In my earlier days we would compare tips on dieting and how to view our burgeoning bodies in the highly placed mirrors of the ward's bathroom. Jenny died of a heart attack whilst having a feeding tube inserted into her throat.

There was another woman with OCD who was constantly washing. After I left the hospital and was in various public toilets in Wellington post or pre throwing up, I would see her, scrubbing and wringing her hands in the communal hand basin.

There was another bulimic whose aunt I would later meet, as she was a receptionist in a massage parlour I worked in.

One of my visitors told me that the great love of my life, Peter Irwin had been in a motorbike accident and was in a nearby ward in the same hospital (needless to say I was in the psychiatric ward). We had had a non-consummated affair on the basis of a shared 'geekdom'. We debated against each other, been on opposing teams of 'It's Academic', an intercollegiate quiz show, and shared kisses. However when I lost weight I lost my geek credibility and Peter backed off as I sailed into pretty girl madness land. Anyway, being in a body cast in a neighbouring ward meant a captive audience to the stream of correspondence I sent him; although he never replied.

When I fought against the regime, the visitors and strolls ceased. I was put on perpetual bed rest. I tried to persuade my family to get me released but they did what they thought was right and listened to the medical establishment.

The ward sister was called Sister Garlic (I jest you not!) Despite being built like a proverbial tank, she was kind and comforted me as I was force fed.

There was also a lovely male nurse who would play chess as we passed the hour after eating I needed to wait until I was allowed to go to the toilet.

Eventually I ran away from the hospital, in my backless hospital gown, moving on shaky thin legs through the streets of Newtown. A nurse who brought me back, seated me on the bed and went to find a doctor; whereupon I promptly fled again.

This time I did get to a friend's house. That night I went to a party. I rang my parents to tell them I was safe. They picked me up in their yellow Datsun Sunny, ostensibly to discuss further strategy, and promptly drove me back to the hospital.

I managed to persuade my parents not to section me. We made an agreement. I had a week to find a flat and resume my studies. We were to embark on a relationship of 'tough love'.

We would still attend the family counselling sessions, but I wasn't to visit them without making an appointment. Apart from an allowance (to cover rent etc as I was too young to receive benefit and was still at school) I was to maintain an independent existence.

Shortly after this they moved to Hong Kong. Whilst I stayed out of hospital in Wellington I spent the next seven or eight years in and out of institutions for a variety of breakdowns, attempted suicides and overdoses.

I even made a few visits to hospitals in Hong Kong. Once it was to have a pregnancy terminated. The second time was to visit a Vietnamese refugee, a very young girl with cancer who had lost her hair and eye brows to chemotherapy. I was showing her some make up tips to cheer her up.

I have had a long-standing relationship with the private hospital, Raffles, in Singapore, due to my mother's chronic obstructive pulmonary disease

In the last week of my mother's life, our family camped out in the ICU in Raffles hospital. I would stand outside in the early hours of the morning, having a cigarette and listening to the call to prayer at a nearby mosque.

My relationship with hospitals in the UK was a very different although drugs proved a common denominator.

I was affiliated with Maudsley psychiatric hospital for my methadone treatment and related counselling sessions.

It was here I found out I was Hep. C positive (initially this was referred to as non Hep A, non Hep B) which wasn't the best present to give my fiancée who had accompanied me on that particular visit.

It was across the road at Kings College Hospital I went when I lost my baby at seven months. I also had the subsequent pregnancy terminated, as the conception was too soon after to the stillbirth.

Since then I have had a long standing but relatively trauma free relationships with my local hospital monitoring and treating my Hep. C and assorted related health problems.

I is for Inheritance

My mother's adoptive parents were very much of a generation that lived simply, didn't get into debt and saved money and assets for their descendants when they died.

I was in my mid teens when my grandfather died. I'd stopped in Blenheim to visit him mid hitchhiking trip around the South Island. I found that the hospital he was in had administered the last rites, but not informed any of my family that he was dying. Perhaps this wasn't so surprising as my mother was so traumatised by abuse suffered at her adoptive parents hands, letting go of them was a closure of sorts; the only way to try and live a semblance of a life.

My mother used the money her father left her to buy a house in Wellington. When the rest of my family left New Zealand they sold the house investing the proceeds with a friend Ross, who later died whilst renovating his pie cart. A rivet gun backfired into his lung. Strangely enough it was friends' of mine who found Ross after this accident and called the ambulance.

Ross did not get on with his family but was very successful at moneymaking ventures. When Ross died his family destroyed his paperwork including his will which contained details about my mother's money, a house he had left to us, as well as a trust set up for his own de-facto wife and her child. All his assets eventually went to his estranged and shrewd family.

My grandfather created a trust fund for my sister and me. We would receive the bulk of when we reached 20. It was a respectable amount (about NZ$30,000). I was able to draw on it prior for clothes and educational needs.

Due to the financial demands that my habitual partying created I became adept at procuring receipts to draw on this trust. I had adopted a nomadic life at this stage, which meant I was unable to work in the parlours and brothels of Wellington, which had previously been my main way of supplementing my income.

When I turned 20 I was living in Dunedin. I immediately booked tickets to Hong Kong to see my family, also London as it seemed the right thing to do.

I hired a van and gathered together a group of friends to drive up to Christchurch where my plane was departing in ten days.

I couldn't drive, so Henry, a friend, was designated driver. Onboard were Matthew, Hazel, Anne Marie, Robert and a few others whose names I can no longer remember. I loaded up with crates of expensive alcohol, pills brought from various friends' prescriptions, and high quality marijuana. We made it as far as the boundaries of Dunedin then crashed the van. We returned to the city and hired a new one.

Initially we were going to stay with friends in Christchurch, but they evicted us due to bad behaviour. So I booked us into a hotel, which also threw us out.

We spent a night or two in the van then stayed in the house of another, more relaxed friend. I had a mushroom trip which made my flight from New Zealand to Hong Kong rather uncomfortable.

Once in Hong Kong I went on a medically supervised withdrawal from opiates. I drank and partied my way through a considerable portion of my money in upmarket nightclubs, and spent my more sober daytime hours training to be a beauty therapist.

Then I went to London and at a party met an Australian man called Stuart. He suggested we go to Spain the next day. On the train to Heathrow I lost my wallet. I spent my time in Europe relying on my new friend's communist sensibilities, and trying to access the remainder of my money, which I had left with my family in Hong Kong.

When we arrived in Berlin, where, due to its divided and isolated status at that time, the only place that I could make a reverse charge phone call was at the Zoo Bahnhoff Railway station. I contacted my parents to be told that they had lost all their/our money in a bit of financial mismanagement.

Thus went the inheritance.

J is for Jimmy (previously known as Hedley)

After I left hospital I moved into a flat in central Wellington, close to the High School which I had planned to attend for my seventh form year.

I found the advertisement for the flat on the Victoria University notice board. The other inhabitants were older than myself and were mostly students.

Paul and Caroline were a couple, both studying English Literature as was another of my flatmates,

Brett was in his final year medicine. Jimmy was simply unemployed.

It was a ramshackle Victorian two story house, and very cheap. I suspect my presence stirred things up a little as aside from being younger than everyone else, I was the only one of my peers who had a flat. My sister and her friends, as well as my own, used to congregate there.

I immediately hit it off with Jimmy (who had changed his name from Hedley as Jimmy was more 'street'). He was closest to my age, background and persona.

As with everyone else in the flat, bar myself and Brett, Jimmy was well over 6ft tall but incredibly thin, with bad skin. He was intelligent with the same interests in art, music and philosophy as me. He adored clothes. He also adored drugs.

A friend of his, Dale, had a father who was in the final stages of terminal cancer. Dale used to steal his father's drugs, then come around to Carrington Street to share and sometimes sell these predominantly opiate based drugs.

At that stage my mother was injecting an experimental drug for PMT. I used to break into my parent's home when they were at work, sift through pockets for change, handbags for pills and skim a few of her needles and syringes (she was so untidy she never noticed).

I had started off using drinking-morphine. It was instant drug love; a key to a lock - finding THE drug that suited me.

From there, via Dale, I progressed to injecting synthetics such as Temgesic and Omnipom.

In-between the opiate times Jimmy and I used to take my mother's pills and some rather nasty allergy tabs that gave vivid hallucinations but made us jumpy, edgy and ill.

We both loved the band The *Birthday Party*; friends would visit, sniff glue then flail around to songs such as 'Fingers Down the Throat of Love' or 'Deep in the Woods a Funeral is Swinging', whilst smashing holes in the walls. Jimmy's particular obsession was *Joy Division*, the lead singer, Ian Curtis, having recently hung himself.

We were both as tortured as only creative, intelligent teenagers could be. We would often dress in our finest, me in a wedding dress perhaps with a full train, him wearing a top hat carrying a cane. We would go out and when we had passed out wake up on his bed after being carried home by one of our giant flatmates.

We went to *avant garde* films, concerts and parties together. We protested nuclear warships coming to New Zealand and once staggered around Wellington spraying the anagram of Ian Curtis, 'I Curtains', around the city.

We did sleep together on one occasion but it was a disaster, not least because we were so thin that our bones clanged together. We were simply friends who loved each other very deeply.

Jimmy's girlfriend, a podgy blond punk called Juliet had real problems with me. She would try to separate us, although initially it made no difference to our relationship. At one point our respective ill health and weight loss became so bad we made a blood pact with each other to live.

I moved out of Carrington Street soon after that. I'd occasionally see Jimmy around but he seemed to be avoiding me. The last time I saw him he actually turned tail and fled when he spotted me. I later found out Juliet had threatened to leave him if he continued to have contact with me.

He hung himself when he was 18.

Jimmy's funeral was Catholic, so his family covered up his cause of death, suicide being then considered a cardinal sin.

This lie disgusted and saddened me. Although I attended another friend's wake a few years later, I refused to go to funerals for the next 20 years. I still hate them.

J is for Jump (ing out of a plane)

I decided to mark the occasion of my seven year clean time Narcotics Anonymous birthday in as dramatic manner as possible. Admittedly I was rather disillusioned with the non-creative, spiritually homogenised path of sobriety that I had taken. So this was also an attempt to shake what had become an unhappy life.

Rather than my old methods of life reconstruction (inappropriate affairs and house wrecking parties) this time around I decided to do a parachute jump to raise a little money for charity. My lover at that time, being afraid of heights, decided to join me.

We did the daylong course, which was to culminate with the actual jump in an old airfield in Devon. The instructor was ex army and covered in Pagan tattoos. Given my own smattering of tattoos indicating Pagan spirituality, we quickly bonded.

By day's end our numbers had dropped considerably as the magnitude of what we were doing hit us. Even the crusty old biker who had received the jump as a birthday present decided it wasn't right for him.

We went up in a small plane without seats or a door. I was to jump out first, the reasoning being if men saw the only woman in the group taking the plunge, their macho instinct would make them less inclined to back out.

I leaped out of the plane forgetting all lessons on technique and safety. As I sailed out the door, the instructor looked out after me and said, 'Oh fuck'.

I went backward under the plane. The chute didn't open but I was so busy enjoying the sound of rushing air in silence and the feeling of empty space, I neglected to open my emergency parachute. That perhaps was a good thing as my primary chute did eventually open.

I landed in the right place, but on my rear, in a less than dignified manner. When I disentangled myself I ran around for some time, elated and exhilarated, neglecting to notice that the backside had been ripped clean from my trousers.

It didn't actually matter.

K is for Kin

The counselling sessions my family attended together for over a year were chaotic and rambling messes. We had two councillors. Raewyn and Tamara, who would flail around with textbook diagnosis allotting blame, encouraging drama, and applauding outbursts.

Eventually my parents went to the local University library and did some research. They realised that I had an eating disorder and our therapists were applying the standard methods of that time in dealing with it (blaming my mother).

In one session it was revealed that I had a half brother. Strangely this revelation, whilst a shock, didn't initially hold much interest for me.

My mother became pregnant at 17 to one of her lecturers at University. As was the way at that time; she was whisked off in the later, visible stages of the pregnancy, to a Nun run home for unwed mothers.

She gave birth to a son who was immediately taken away, any further contact between mother and child was forbidden.

The adoptive father kept in touch with my mother for some years, with news and images of her son Vincent's progress. He alluded to his wife being very insecure about the possibility of my mother one day appearing to reclaim her child.

This contact with my mother stopped after five or so years; my mother was so caught up in her own family and life, she didn't pursue it.

Weirdly, we actually knew the man who had fathered this child; my sister and I were close to his family. When I realised that I would be leaving and most likely not returning to New Zealand, I decided to initiate a search for my brother.

I contacted an organisation called Jigsaw who mediated between adopted children and their birth families, to help me find Vincent.

About a year later I was about to depart from the country, but no inroads seemed to have been made by Jigsaw in the matter. I tracked Vincent down myself and, much to my shame, rang his family home.

Now I am not someone who had many regrets, but the way I handled this situation was and is one of my major life mistakes. I was coming down from a weeklong mushroom party. Any sense of logic; consideration and sensitivity were lost to me. Vincent's sister answered the phone. I asked to speak to Vincent, telling her that I was his half sister.

She started crying, her mother took the phone off her and started abusing me, calling my mother a whore and such like.

Some years later Vincent did contact my mother. They talked and eventually met although contact lapsed as his adopted mother became very uncomfortable with the relationship.

I talked to him once. We seemed to have similar interests, temperaments, bouts of introversion and depression. I never pursued further contact. When my mother died I decided not to track him down to inform him.

K is for Kite

When I was eleven I started attending Sacred Heart College in Wellington. I had already been to 15 schools and had never lived in one place long enough to really settle and explore the possibility of having friends.

My five years at Sacre Coeur, combined with puberty and experiments in chemical, emotional and social boosting gave me space for the first time, to make clumsy attempts at mixing with a world outside myself.

I made several close friends. I gradually came further out of my shell and mixed within a culture that was about cars, motorbikes and rugby.

Our garb, when not in school uniform with its blazer, hat, tie and gloves, were jeans and sweatshirts, or for dances, high heels and tight straight skirts.

At 14 and in the flush of my first major weight loss my mother sent me to 'The Academy of Elegance', a New Zealand adaptation of a Swiss finishing school. In many ways it was horribly conventional with its lessons in how to tie neck scarves in interesting combinations of knots, apply makeup, and walk without slouching. Despite the mainstream pretensions of the academy, I came away with a greater confidence in expressing my interest in clothes and self.

I had my long hair cut in a graduated bob and started to experiment with my appearance. I met a group of people who were not connected with my school friends or their partners. These new acquaintances appeared to be different, exciting and more on my own wavelength.

None of these people went to Catholic schools, they had moneyed, slightly bohemian backgrounds where books and the arts were valued and politics were left leaning.

Yes, there may have been a whiff of pretension and high camp about it. *Brideshead Revisited* had just been released as a TV series, which had a major influence on the fashion sense of some of my new acquaintances. In my elation with my life's new possibilities I was careless about retaining contact with my long term, once close school friends, but I started to blossom.

I was taken to a black and white ball at the Band Rotunda on Oriental Parade in Wellington on the back of a new boyfriend's motorbike. I was wearing a black floor length 1930s lace gown, and waltzed to the music of an accordion player.

I learned to fly a kite and ride a skateboard. I attended cutting edge art productions, was driven around in my lover's tiny Fiat Bambino and met people whose mothers read and worked rather than cleaned the house or looked pristine for PTA meetings.

My English teacher submitted without my knowledge, a short story of mine to a competition. I won the PEN international young writers award. I received a small cheque, some media recognition and was due to have an official presentation at the New Zealand houses of Parliament (The Beehive) by the author Thomas Keneally.

Photographs taken of me were left at a modelling agency and I was chosen to be in an advertisement for 'Ginger Nut' biscuits on television. Due to a late night I messed up the dates and times of my appearance, arriving at Avalon Studios for the filming looking very jaded. I didn't present myself in the most professional light.

I was going out with a leonine young man, and a gay antiques dealer. We would fall into bed in a tangle of ornate clothing and smooth young limbs; a beautiful and decadent triad.

I still remember walking home from parties at this golden boy's house (whilst his parents were in Europe) through the deserted streets of Wellington as the sun was coming up.

In those days the coffee bars would have their deliveries left outside in the very early morning, so I could filch a bottle of milk to whet my pallet as I watched the streets being cleaned.

This awakening only lasted six months or so. Then I was put in psychiatric care. When I came out of hospital I was more frantic and less accepting. Gradually I realised that these wonderful golden people were not quite as open and bohemian as I thought. Word would come back to me of gossip and judgements. Whilst I retained my love of dressing up and glamour, I moved on to find new friends; friends who lived in the frenetic moment, with no dreams of an affluent or established future.

I tucked the invite to the PEN awards presentation in a school textbook with some notes of an essay that was due, but never finished. I never went back to that school; I lost the invite and didn't make the ceremony.

L is for Law (or lack of)

The reader may have ascertained by this point in my narrative, that my morality when younger, was not the most conventional.

Perhaps because I was brought up within environments coloured by fundamentalist Catholicism and a family with obvious mental health issues, the morality they transmitted was suspect. I was a slow learner when it came to adhering to the proverbial law of the land.

I never felt any guilt or shame for my work as a prostitute and mercifully managed to avoid getting arrested, but my drug and alcohol abuse brought me into closer contact with the courts.

I lived in flats where it wasn't unusual to be searched by the police. On one occasion I came out of our living room to see a stream of police pouring up our stairs. I tried to run to the kitchen to warn my compatriots who were cooking up a home bake of heroin from Paracetemol. A policeman intercepted me and deliberately broke my fingers by slamming a door on my hand.

The New Zealand police force at that time tended to be old school, especially in the smaller towns of the South Island, often with a background in the military or navy. They could be tough, sometimes brutal, occasionally fair and even compassionate.

The laws around drugs at that time were murky. Needles were illegal and due to an assiduous customs service heroin was rare. Most opiate addicts were resourceful and knowledgeable chemists.

When I first moved to Dunedin a group of friends were gathered in an empty house brewing up San Pedro Cactus. I had just left when the police raided them.

Thirteen of my friends were arrested and charged, but due to the vague laws surrounding preparation of this plant, they were released.

The Dunedin courtrooms were a sociable place. They were in the centre of town and we used to pop in between visits to the drug clinic or the pub to see who was appearing before the court that day, and who might be 'going down'. The possibility of someone going to prison necessitated at least a week of hard core and nihilistic partying before sentencing.

One very pretty male friend, Shonnie, hung himself in the holding cells in Nelson when he knew he would have to serve another prison sentence.

I was driving with a group of friends to Wellington in an old Wolsey when we were pulled over in a small town and searched. In the car boot they found spoons, needles and various remnants of our recent raid of a poppy patch where we had dried, cooked and injected the milk extracted from the plants.

At that point I had an opiate habit (I think I was the only one of my number who did, my companions being only occasional users). Once the police realised this they integrated my discomfort into their interrogation techniques. I was put in a very cold cell, with no blankets, for a day and a night and taken out every three hours or so to be aggressively questioned.

I pleaded not guilty so needed to commute back and forth to Timaru.One time I underwent the five hour journey on the back of a 125cc motorbike withdrawing and with piles, which was hellish to say the least. I changed my plea to guilty, the case transferred back to Dunedin where the file was lost and I got off with a warning; unlike my friends who all received convictions.

Over the years I had various brushes with the New Zealand law, and the occasional night in the cells or court appearance. I managed to avoid a conviction, which was a minor miracle and a great gift in my later, more respectable years.

Living in England, apart from the occasional squatting incident, I generally managed to avoid legal problems. Small time class A drug users were generally left alone as arresting them was more labour intensive than it was worth. When places that I was living were raided, the police would leave any drug paraphernalia or residue untouched - HIV may have contributed to this supposed indifference.

A different perspective of the legal system was provided to me when I was working in the Herne Hill pub that hosted the yearly Peckham Rye CID Christmas party. A week before the event local traders and businessmen in a variety of guises, started bringing appreciative and lavish gifts to contribute to the party. Crates of good wine and cartons of excellent whiskey being the tip of the well lubricated occasion.

It was a raucous affair, although I was incredibly uneasy working the bar. I started the late shift after an Alex Chilton concert, and was very, very stoned.

However no one seemed to notice.

M is for : Mushrooms

M is for Mushrooms (of the magic variety)

Now mushrooms were not my 'thing' they didn't suit me at all, especially in my later stages of full on addiction where hallucinogens bring on withdrawal. Trying to inject whilst tripping is an incredibly unpleasant experience. However mushrooms are abundant and easy to find in New Zealand so I took them, took them many times.

One especially memorable mushroom experience was at a party on a peninsular on the outskirts of Dunedin. It was in a large wooden community centre built on a spit, surrounded by water. In this odd and isolated place a masked ball had been organised, invites sent to the members of our clan, which was scattered throughout New Zealand.

Masks were compulsory, as was consumption of huge quantities of mushrooms. If you weren't masked when you arrived you were held down and had one painted on your face.

The party was wild and atavistic. I burned out quickly as I wasn't physically strong at that point in time. I went to lie in a friend's car until someone felt inclined to drive us back to Dunedin (drink driving laws in the countryside of New Zealand were not rigorously enforced at that time).

The car park had become a place of horror.

Those that the mushrooms had stripped to the core of their base selves were prowling around the car park, armed with pieces of wood looking to fight or ... something.

I spent the rest of the night hiding under a blanket on the floor of the back seat in absolute terror.

M is for the Music

Music was a huge part of my life although I never learned to play any instrument and can only sing in one, off kilter note. My mother was a serious, very talented musician until shock treatment blasted away her ability and knowledge; perhaps one of the reasons she actively discouraged my sister and I from learning to play any instrument.

Initially my life's background music was jazz (my father's choice) and classical (my mother's) with lots of religious ditties and hymns thrown in from school to be performed for my grandmother or elderly relatives.

When my father left, we moved into a commune. We were suddenly surrounded by the contemporary music of the 1960s and 1970s from Led Zeppelin, Genesis, Neil Young and The Allman Brothers

Everyone seemed to have a guitar and/or a set of bongos. There were many joyful, impromptu music and dance sessions.

One happy albeit strange memory was of my sister and I tucked into bed in a small room wallpapered in eyes cut from magazines, with lips from the same sources covering the ceiling. We listened to bedtime stories from a wild eyed family friend, the sounds of Randy Newman's 'Sail Away' album providing background sounds.

When I was eleven my mother, her boyfriend Ian, my sister and myself went to the three day Sweetwaters Music festival at the top of the North Island.

Not able to cope with my mother's tossing away of her clothing for the duration of the festival, my sister and I did our own thing. We saw *Elvis Costello*, *INXS* and *Split Enz* amongst others and had a wonderful time. I had my first toke on a joint, and developed a crush on a man who let my sister ride on his shoulders so she could see the bands.

It was a traditional hippy environment; with children and dogs roaming free; stalls selling lentil mush and not much else. Two young children wandering around were enveloped into a very safe, loving, if rather stoned, crowd.

I started going to concerts on my own soon after, from the more mainstream such as *Cheap Trick* or *Tom Petty and the Heartbreakers* to the new and edgy such as *The Cure*, *Siouxse and the Banshees* and *The Jam*.

Siouxse and the Banshees was a bit of a wash out for me. I was having a very visual mushroom trip and the throwing around of the bodies on the dance floor was intensely disturbing in this state. At one point one of the audience spat at the singer. Siouxse swung her microphone stand at the culprit in retaliation but the intended recipient ducked; I had a drugged slow motion vision burned on my retina of the stand connected with an innocent member of the audience.

I left *The Police* concert as a mixture of drink and my sister's asthma inhaler brought on a frightening series of palpitations that only immersion in the fountain outside Wellington's Town Hall was able to stop.

Mid teens I immersed myself in the darkness of *Joy Division* and the primal *Birthday Party* (to whom we could get free tickets if we swapped drugs with the organisers). I developed a liking for musicians as lovers.

If a man was skilled at making music, I was smitten for a time (generally a short one) but as my own partying was rather intense I quickly bonded with musicians who had a propensity for hard living.

There was Dragon, who was an amazing guitarist but ended up trying to strangle me, as I wasn't the most faithful of girlfriends. He was exceptionally possessive.

A brief fling with Lindsay, who killed himself soon afterwards, led me to be introduced to his friend, flatmate and fellow band member Martyn, whom I was to eventually to spend many years with (well five, which on my relationship scale is long term commitment).

At one stage a technician from *Flying Nun* tried to teach me to use a mixing desk, as I was obviously creative. There were no female mixers around at that time; however every lesson degenerated into a stoner or drink session. I ended up having a relationship with my tutor that ended badly (again due to my short concentration span and infidelity).

There were many, many more musician lovers, but gradually I realised my own creative abilities. I burned out from the drug involvement in that sphere, then backed off from the New Zealand music scene.

I moved for a second time to England inspired by a desire to see *The Pixies* live. I kept up with the NME magazine subscriptions and music in all the classic venues of the time such as *The Marquee*, *Brixton Academy*, *Ronnie Scots*, *Dingwalls* and *The Mean Fiddler* until my drug habits swamped any other interests and took all my money.

I think my swansong was seeing *Alex Chilton* perform; a rare and wonderful opportunity that I was too stoned to remember or appreciate.

It took many years of mundane sobriety before I was able to relax enough to resume my passionate affair with sound.

N is for Nona

As a member of the self-titled, creative junkie, outsider class of society, I mixed with a broad spectrum of people united only by an interest in drugs and an inability to fit into mundane society.

These disparate groups included criminals, Mongrel Mob gang members, the mentally ill, as well as my own peers of drug addicted arty types.

Our meeting places were the courthouse; pubs, the drug clinic, and the waiting rooms of various doctors known for writing scripts for desirable drugs.

The first time I met Nona I was outside a central Dunedin bar waiting for an ambulance to arrive, whilst tending to a boyfriend who had been badly beaten and slashed by the bouncers.

Nona was what was known at that time in New Zealand as a street kid, the moniker applied to young Maori kids who were often homeless and used glue or solvents as their drug of choice.

Nona had Scottish as well as Maori ancestry; for a while she wore her clan's kilt and later had the moko tattooed on her chin in the traditional, hammer and chisel, manner. She was wild and wonderful, and often very badly behaved. There was some justification in her behaviour as she came from a hellish background and was still very young

At one stage she became psychotic, although I suspect this was a temporary result of the drugs, rather than any actual mental condition such as schizophrenia. She became interested in Christianity, obsessed with the concept of possession. She went on a rampage, destroying artwork by others and myself which she decided were evil. I was working on a set of murals on canvas of dancing skeletons based on a Totentanz theme. She decimated them.

However memory of this destruction faded quickly. I would quite happily chat to her when I ran into her at several of our social hot spots.

She crashed for a while at one of the flats I briefly lived in. I have a vivid memory of a flatmate of mine, Chris, boiling down Gees Linctus to drink and lecturing her on her own choice of unhealthy drugs.

On one occasion I was picked up by police for an outstanding conviction that I was avoiding dealing with. I met her in the holding cells. A member of the CID (Criminal Investigation Department) harassed her so she had set fire to the building that housed their offices. She probably would have got away with it but she returned to retrieve a bottle of vodka she had left at the scene then stayed to enjoy the crowd atmosphere that was developing. She was so overly loud in her appreciation of the spectacle to the point of being suspicious enough to arrest.

She was well known at Dunedin Police Station which had very traditional old concrete cells, painted in peeling green, covered in graffiti with miserable, rusty wire sprung, and thin mattresses on the beds. She managed to avoid having her tobacco and matches confiscated so we spent some time chatting, smoking and having a good catch up.

After I was released I lost track of Nona. I think she must have gone to prison for a long time; arson is a heavy, heavy crime and the building concerned being the home of the CID made it more so.

O is for : Overdose

O is for Overdose

My first overdose was when I was four years old. It was on the less than illustrious, and not at all hardcore combination of Haliborange vitamin C pills, fluoride tablets and assorted tranquillisers.

At that point my mother, sister and I were living in a brick terrace house very close to my grandmother, which probably explains why my mother was on even more medication than usual. My father had disappeared on one of his many bids to escape the family madness. I think my mother had just come out of a stint in the psychiatric hospital where she had the ECT that they prescribed at that time for severe postnatal depression, as well as the propensity for being a highly intelligent and creative woman who was not content with her lot.

The pills were kept at the top of a kitchen cabinet, so a complex climb was necessary for me to get to them, all the more amazing and determined a feat, as I was by no stretch of the imagination, an athletic child. I had my stomach pumped but I have no recollection of that auspicious occasion.

Many years passed before I had my next major overdose although there were more minor incidents where I took too much of some substance or other. I came to, wandering naked, deaf and confused two days post drug taking (heroin) or hitchhiking around New Zealand clutching a *Times* magazine to ground me to reality a month after over consumption (mushrooms) or miss an historic David Bowie outdoor concert because the 10s of 1000s of spectators had transformed into primordial sea anemones, reality had disappeared and I had lost consciousness (San Pedro cactus).

When I was 24 I had returned to New Zealand after yet another attempt to give up drugs, hoping to start living a motivated and sober life. I came back to a husband who was an active heroin user, with flatmates and friends who were the same, meaning that my noble intentions didn't last long.

My husband at that time was engaged in a string of robberies of chemist shops and the city's medical school. That particular night I had tried to stop him lurching off to commit another burglary.

We still had an impressive array of drugs on hand from the recent robbery of a detox unit, predominantly barbiturates and Heminevrin, neither of which I was fond of unless I was withdrawing and desperate for relief, but Martyn decided he wanted something more opiate based.

I tried to stop him but he shoved me aside and wove off into the night. For some reason being shoved aside seemed to trigger all the feelings I had had prior about being worthless. It reiterated how bad my life had become. So while Martyn was off on his quest I started, in a paced out methodical and correct manner, to consume large quantities of drugs with the intention of killing myself.

From what I understand when Martyn came back with his spoils he found me unconscious, having major seizures. Another friend, Leanne, came around and found Martyn sitting next to me, occasional shooting at me with a slug gun to try to revive me, swigging from a bottle of Marsala.

Leanne and her partner called an ambulance and I was declared dead on arrival when I reached the hospital. I was eventually resuscitated, remaining in a coma for a week. My family, who were living in Hong Kong, were contacted and told that I would probably die but if I did live, I had been clinically dead long enough to have irreversible and severe brain damage.

My conscious mind came to at what would have been my second day in a coma. I had none of the proverbial near death experiences, but instead my brain started working in a body that was wracked with pain and discomfort. Apart from hearing, and physical sensation, it had no vision, control of senses or ability to move.

I fought so hard to let the nurses and my friend sitting beside me holding my hand know that I was alive...but I couldn't.

My brain switched off again. When it resumed cognitive function, I was conscious having regained use of my senses and ability to move.

When I left intensive care I was transferred briefly to a psych unit, medicated for inhalation pneumonia then released. I immediately started injecting drugs. Shortly afterwards I left New Zealand, and haven't been back since.

I suppose this category should also mention the overdoses of others, something which I am loath to do as the list is way too long.

I was a dab hand at C.P.R., which although probably not text book, was effective. I remember coming into a room where a friend had O.D.'d to find everyone gathered around him but unwilling to resuscitate as he was a carrier for Hepatitis B. I did it and he recovered to enjoy many more years of active addiction.

There were less direct forms of overdoses where friends were so drunk they passed out, allowing a candle to combust the room/ house where everyone died.

Saturday night paralysis was another consequence of imbibing too much. One friend passed out whilst lying on his arm in the police holding cells in Dunedin. Luckily he didn't lose his arm despite the blood flow being cut off for a long period of time but for many months afterwards his arm had a strange metallic splint, which could be manipulated to exercise the dead limb. I don't think he ever recovered full movement.

I lost over 20 friends around one Christmas when Dunedin drug clinic cut off everyone's methadone script. There was a panic robbery of a local vet's clinic resulting in many, many friends overdosing on horse tranquilliser.

It is too painful to catalogue the deaths through overdose of friends or acquaintances that time and necessity has made faceless, so I will just mention a few of those closest to me.

John Holman whom I loved dearly although didn't sleep with, a wonder in itself only allotted to those I cared for most! John couldn't stand my husband Martyn, so when John and his girlfriend moved out of the house we shared; John only visited me on Saturday, when Martyn was doing Periodic Detention for some crime or other.

John Holman died of an overdose, probably self-administered. His body sat in a chair at a party, facing a bay window looking out onto a busy footpath for many, many hours before anyone realised he was dead. His long leather coat disappeared within hours of his death.

I was asked to speak at his Quaker memorial service. I cannot remember what I said; did I ask how someone can die of loneliness yet still have so many people turn up at their wake?

I didn't attend his funeral.

John O Brien was my first lover in recovery from addiction, the first person I had sex with without the aid of drugged or alcoholic distance. It was an odd, emotional relationship but John's insecurity was fed by putting me firmly down; so after a year or so I left although I still loved him deeply.

From a distance I watched his brother die from an overdose. At one stage I needed to get a court order to stop John visiting me at odd hours of the night, well drugged. I reached this stage of zero tolerance when John tried to run down my then current partner with a car.

One day I received a letter from John saying he was clean, that he still loved me, and was going to come and get me back on his new motorbike, him fit and resplendent in leather trousers. That night I received a phone call from John's mother saying that his body had been found, dead from overdose, in a local public toilet, trousers still around his ankles when he had been taking a last hit to his groin.

P is for Pills

My mother was very much a woman of her time; creative, intelligent, damaged and conflicted. The system consequently took the proscribed and prescribed route for her; medication, lots of it combined with the occasional stint in a psych ward and blast of ECT.

I was brought up by a woman who was heavily medicated. Colourful diet pills to keep her weight down, pills for anxiety and sleeping, pills for relaxation, pills for getting out of the house.

The most entertaining bedtime stories were in the Quaalude days however as anti depressants evolved and the benzo-diazapams were scaled down, a much happier woman emerged.

I was born with a hole in the heart perhaps due to my mother's use of Stemetil for her vomiting phobia; my sister was born premature, severely underweight, and with asthma perhaps for the same reason although that could also be attributed to my mother's chain smoking. I can only thank god that she narrowly missed being prescribed thalidomide.

By the time I was eleven I was crawling under my mother's bed or rifling through her handbags to come away with handfuls of loose and forgotten pills. I would have pill parties with friends of mine from school. Many was the Monday when we would all find ourselves in sick bay at school trying to piece together from broken memories, what we had done over the weekend.

When my family moved to Hong Kong a friend of mine bought the house and had a huge housewarming party fuelled with the 100s of pills they had found when they lifted the carpets of their new home.

P is for : Prostitution

P is for Prostitution

How I started working in the sex industry, and ended up staying there for over ten years was seemingly triggered by a single innocuous event. However it was actually the culmination of years of experiences which influenced my views on my sense of self, my body and my sexuality.

My best friend at my school from ages 10-12 was a Hungarian girl called Maria. Her family were immigrants to New Zealand in the 1970s. Like me, Maria was precociously well developed, oversized and highly intelligent with a family lifestyle which tended to confirm her school status as an alien and outsider. The school, Mt Carmel, was small, nun taught and epitomised the traditional, old style Catholic approach.

I was the only child attending at that time who came from a one parent family (although that changed within a very few years). I was living with my mother and sister in a hippy commune filled with politically aware radical students, music, dogs, and the occasionally mentally ill person. Murals of the game of life covered the wall of the stairwell of the large ramshackle Victoria house.

Maria's parents were working-class Hungarians. Her father was wont to wander around the house in Speedos eating whole chillies, which was a disconcerting sight as he had been a weight lifter and when he stopped lifting the muscle changed to fat...and a lot of it. The mother was plump, smiling and submissive. They had an expensive car, large colour television and other high tech, gadgets, which were all a rarity in New Zealand at that time.

Initially the father had worked as a road builder when he came to New Zealand but he was a shrewd business man and having spotted a niche in the market he launched a series of what were to become very successful massage parlours.

Thus visiting Maria meant meeting strange woman of a type I had never come across before, women with rough voices, crude language, skimpy clothing and tattoos, tattoos especially being a very rare thing in mainstream society at that time.

Birthday parties for Maria were high cost events. She would invite over 30 school friends, but most parents would refuse to allow their children to come. So generally there would only be two or three guests overwhelmed by mounds of incredible food and lavish entertainment.

I always denied that Maria's father's business was anything beyond simple massage parlours. Sometimes Maria and I would go to one of them for a saunas or spa pool; always in the daytime when there were no clients around.

By my early teens Maria and I saw less of each other as my secondary school (another old fashioned Catholic school but this one with pretensions) refused to allow Maria to attend for 'moral reasons'.

I always had sideline employment at that point to make money. Baby sitting, painting and decorating, digging old bottles from under houses to sell, helping out at Trade Fairs or working in auction rooms, being just some of my money making ventures.

I saw a job advertised as a receptionist in a Bath House/Massage Parlour in central Wellington. It looked promising as a financial source for some rather stylish blue suede pixie boots that I had decided were a sartorial necessity.

I managed to persuade my mother to drop me off at said bathhouse, although she did say that she thought the job possibly wasn't appropriate. I had my interview. Although I was only 14-15, I was tall and very well developed. I had lost some of my excess poundage but was still overweight, not having yet embarked on the more excessive dieting I later became lost in, although I was already bulimic.

The man who interviewed me was middle age, short and balding. We were alone in the building, as 11am was not standard visiting time for massage parlours clientele.

He showed me around the hot pools general layout, then insisted on giving me a massage whilst simultaneously undermining my esteem by making remarks about my excess weight.

Then he had sex with me.

I cannot even remember what my sexual experience was then; probably a lot, but as the passive participant, as I suspect most insecure women of that age are.

Was it rape?

I don't know. I didn't consider it as such. I never went back but took the $40 he gave me and bought my boots which I had good wear out of.

My eating disorder took off at that point so for a period of time I was out of prostitution and in the less lucrative loop of being counselled in psychiatric care instead. However I did return to the sex industry a year or so later when I started working in various other massage parlours in Wellington.

It took a few days learning the ropes; how to fold towels in the traditional hostess way of three even sections; carry an evening bag with 'equipment' in it, give a massage in a fast, basic and flirtatious way before enquiring whether 'extras' were required in an ambiguous yet clear manner.

My first client managed to persuade me that he shouldn't pay as he hadn't ejaculated but after that I made money, and a lot of it. This money paid for fantastic clothes, drugs, alcohol and binging food supplies, before I left the business for a while. However this sort of work is addictive as is the capacity for earning large amounts of cash in a very short time. I started working in other parlours, before eventually settling at an established bathhouse at 54 Ghuznee Street.

I stayed there for quite a while. I had friends who also worked there and the place was relatively well run. The owner went out with a high up police detective so it seemed safe. When a co-worker of mine, Sue, was raped and beaten on an 'out call', the matter was dealt with by the police but out of the eye of legality...I mean how can you rape a prostitute?

They had a Doberman pinscher as a guard dog, which was kept in a walled courtyard outside their kitchen. Originally this poor creature had been owned by members of the gang, The Mongrel Mob. Its body was covered in scars from cigarette burns and knife wounds.

A friend of mine started going out with the brothel owner's son, and was looking after the dog for a while. I went to visit her. When she opened the door it attacked me, going for the crotch as those dogs are trained to do, but luckily I was wearing disco tights and its teeth slipped so little damage was done.

I had friends who worked in other parlours but I always thought they were older and harder than me. Most had habits or were heavy drinkers with poly addictions.

There were fantastic parties and waterbeds were de rigueur amongst many working girls at that time. My money invariably went on fabulous clothes from high end boutiques and consumables.

I generally worked the dayshift as I wasn't tough enough for the night work. These dayshifts tended to be quieter than the nights, unless the boats were in. We would sit in the lounge awaiting clients, watching Prisoner Cell Block H and gossiping.

Aside from the occasional flock of Japanese sailors (fast short and frenetic bursts of sex), there was one chap who was too well endowed to have sex with his wife (that required wriggling around a bit to accommodate his girth). There were foot fetishists, a survivor from Auschwitz who owned a Konditerie that made the most amazing European confectionaries that he would bring together with gifts of underwear for me; and an anonymous stream of ordinary and faceless men.

I wasn't suited to the BDSM that some of the women made their forte, which was a pity as it seemed an easier route.

Many of us had rules, no kissing, or girl on girl or oral. Those in relationships would tend to maintain these boundaries so that they had something special that only occurred within their relationship.

I had some relationships whilst I was working but no really committed ones. Non-commitment was a constant in my life so I cannot say if it had anything to do with my work. I was as promiscuous before I worked in this sphere as I was during and after.

The sex act meant little to me on an emotional level, although I enjoyed it as a physical act.

I had a few incidents when I was hitchhiking when I would give sexual favours for money and it never really affected me. The morality of sex and money didn't bother me although I found my peers from my earlier days working in this field (middle class left wing school friends and such like) judged me terribly and cruelly.

I gradually moved away from this social circle into more hard core partying realms where I wasn't alone in my 'career' choice. The money it brought into our gatherings was much appreciated.

Of course there were horrible incidents where I was hurt or raped or abused but the drugs were an aid in coping with those.

I had a break for several years, aside from the occasional one off incident, before I resumed working again a legalised brothel in Melbourne. The Greek Mafia supposedly owned this place, which was very strictly run with high security and care for the women that worked there.

We had regular medical checks, paid a bond when we started, always have immaculate make up and wore suitable stockings/suspender belt type underwear. No shaving of one's legs in the hot pool whilst under the influence, as a friend in mine in one parlour had done.

This was well into the hedonistic, materialistic 80s by this point. We were an upmarket clean establishment with a plethora of attractive women with appeal to various tastes; our clients were often young good looking businessmen with no time for relationships, or touring musicians, who would come in with cocaine and book private rooms and several women to party with.

I then met someone who was to be a great, if very flawed love of my life. I left this parlour and moved back to New Zealand to be loved and in love in a grand and passionate way ... until it went horribly and dramatically wrong of course.

Q is for Quiz Show

I was in my early teens when an ambitious television executive dreamed up an intercollegiate version of University Challenge to be shown on New Zealand prime time television. Erskine College, despite being an expensive and exclusive private school, didn't have the highest academic standards. The assembled team comprised of me as Captain (in my bespectacled, overweight, tooth braced and less than photogenic days) and two other girls. We were seated at the top of a rather rickety triangular structure that wobbled ominously when one was leaping up and down trying to produce an answer from the aethyr.

Our team didn't get beyond the first heat. I never saw the programme although apparently my braces reflected rather magnificently under the spotlights.

R is for Rehab

In my younger days I had frequent internments in 'mental institutions' for my various problems. However by my early 20s the focus shifted towards treatment of drug and alcohol dependency.

My first formal in-house detox was in Dartford Kent for opiate addiction.

This was in an annex of the main hospital and in a very old asylum, complete with sliding peepholes over the doors of the individual cells we slept in.

I did the Narcan detox, got to know the staff, but ended up back there a year later to be treated for alcoholism and speed addiction.

In those days there was a degree of enmity between the drug addicts who sat on one side of the room, and the alcoholics (red noses) who sat on the other. The alcoholics often were scratching due to nerve damage, were bloated and had memory lapses. The drug addicts had running noses, would sneeze and whinge a lot and were very thin.

The meals were provided by the hospital, but there was also a small kitchen stocked with biscuits and ingredients for making hot drinks and sandwiches. Invariably this place was bustling with activity from the clients who over the years had spent all their money on drugs and or alcohol, rather than food.

We would have group counselling sessions in a room with reinforced glass, as a chair or two would often end up being thrown around.

Despite my shift in status with my second admission, I still hung out with the more 'hip' junkies. I bonded with a paramedic called Brian; a huge man who had worked on some of the biggest and most traumatic disasters in London including the Clapham Junction train crash. Brian had been in many rehabilitation centres for alcoholism and sex addiction, but had later shifted to using opiates that he would steal from the hospitals where he worked.

Brian and I would flirt and make plans to meet up when we were well. Although by this second visit to the unit I knew that my life had become unliveable if I continued in the same manner as before. I was homeless, but had been staying with a speed dealer who let me have unlimited access to his drugs.

I worked in a local, hard drinking pub, which opened at eight in the morning. I would start each day with speed dissolved in milk, as my nose couldn't take the inhalation any more, then antidepressants, methadone and whiskey. I would top up with the alcohol as the day progressed.

I had lost touch with my family but somehow they had tracked me down and sent me a ticket to join them in Singapore to sort myself out. I couldn't even get it together to use the ticket.

My final drunken swan song was being raped in a men's urinal in the pub I worked in then getting banned from drinking there (in the pub not the urinal) although I still kept my job.

All this time I kept in touch with the drug and alcohol councillor I had been assigned to when I went on a methadone programme. He eventually persuaded me that it was time to return to the detox unit.

A few days before I was due to leave the unit to go to a women's only rehab in the middle of the Kentish countryside, I went to gather some of my possessions from my ex husband, Geoff's house. Within hours I had been to the pawnshop, scored speed and was drunk.

I shacked up at my speed dealer's house then lost consciousness, coming to in a hotel in Brands Hatch with Brian who had left the unit just before me.

Apparently I had taken an overdose of drugs stolen from my speed dealer friend, then rung Brian. Given his previous occupation he had no problem resuscitating me, before driving me from the hotel he had taken me to recover, to Iden Manor Rehabilitation Centre in Kent.

All of this was a black out for me though which I found out about later. I never saw Brian again.

I was in the hospital room of Iden Manor for some time.

This institution was partially funded by the Catholic Church (although the centre was non denominational in approach) partially by the government. It was unusual in its philosophy as aside from being women only, it was fuelled by the belief that the addict or alcoholic should be loved into recovery.

We had our own rooms, beautiful grounds and although technically our stay was for six months, some older women had been there for years.

It was a tragic yet wonderful place. Women died there, children were born there.

We had daily group counselling session, and weekly individual ones. There were never more than 15 women there, aside from some of the long term residents whose families had abandoned them. We were all considered to be at the proverbial 'rock bottom'.

I went to a reunion many years later and heard of companions of that earlier time, who died after leaving, or had relapsed and now had 'wet brain'. I felt incredibly sad that this place was closing due to lack of funding.

After Iden Manor I went to a secondary treatment centre in Bristol that was more specifically focused on self harm, eating disorders and learning to live in the world on a very basic level so we were also taught cooking/bill management and self care skills.

The women here were different than those at Iden Manor. They were younger and there were a greater proportion of drug users.

There was a junkie from Glasgow with some of the most awful scars from abscesses caused by injecting that I had ever seen. In Scotland they had changed the formula for Temazapam aka footballs, so they couldn't be injected but drug users still did. It resulted in awful infections and sometimes loss of limbs.

My first day there I was in a group that discussed one of our member's rape and abuse by her brother from ages 7 to 15. Later groups had similar and sometimes even more painful topics.

Several of my companions there became so anxiety ridden when they left, they became agoraphobic. As far as I know they still live isolated lives, reliant on large amounts of medication.

I was there for three months and as this was also a women's only environment, by the time I moved to Bath for a year in a dry house, I was completely fear ridden about being around men.

I was also institutionalised after being in controlled, regimented and closed environments for over a year and a half continuously, and sporadically for nearly 15 years.

What does being institutionalised entail?

Well for me it brought with it a lot of fear, especially once I left the dry house. I had lived in rule dominated surroundings for so long that spontaneity frightened me and sometimes brought on anxiety attacks.

When I moved into my first flat, I lived in one room for months as I was unable to cope with having a living room AND a bedroom.

I drew up my own structure for each day, gradually pushing my boundaries, working through the terror of breaking the rules I had been indoctrinated to follow.

Initially I became very depressed. Occasionally I yearned for the thing I had possessed in my more wild times; the ability to act spontaneously.

S is for Saint Jude

When my mother left New Zealand she gave a small Wellington based Catholic Church, a long standing donation for candles to be lit and daily prayers said for me, to St Jude the patron saint of the hopeless and despairing.

S is for Santa Claus

Due to another period of turbulence within my delicate family infrastructure I was staying with my grandparents in Blenheim.

I was an isolated child, but times in Blenheim were particularly lonely. My grandparents were middle aged when they had adopted my mother, so they were very old when I was a child. Their peers were also elderly, many working in some capacity or other within the local Catholic Church.

In my time there I went to a school where the nuns were well acquainted with my grandmother and her good deeds. I would visit friends of my grandparents, stand by the piano and sing hymns for them in my distinctive monotone. I would occasionally accompany my grandfather on the back of his huge pushbike to the local rubbish dump, and went to many church services.

However I spent most of my time in the parlour hiding behind a green velvet armchair, away from the terrifying sepia toned images of the agonies of Christ, the collection boxes in the kitchen with a picture of a large bellied, huge eyed starving Biafra child on it, or holy and forbidding images of nuns and 'good girls' like St Theresa. I'd read books that had belonged to my mother as a child. These were generally archaic encyclopaedias, holy tracts, or tales of good but feisty girls such as *Anne of Green Gables.*

On one visit to the playground at the rear of the house where due to fear of injury I stuck to wandering around the trees and plants in the surrounding park. I had to avoid the chain swings which my grandmother maintained could twist around a child's neck and strangle them, the slides which resulted in cracked open heads if you fell off, or the roundabouts which had many horrific accidents on them.

I was suddenly besieged by a hoard of children who caught me up with them as they surged towards a descending helicopter. The 'copter landed and Santa Claus emerged with a large sack of presents and proceeded to call out children's names, then presented the child in question with a gift.

I watched this wonder for a while then he called my name.

I hurried forward, entranced by this miracle and hugged the gift to me...until an adult came up to me and said that they were sorry but I was the wrong 'Charlotte' and took the unwrapped parcel away from me.

S is for Santa Claus (second coming)

When I lived in Queenstown, I once saw Santa Claus come across Lake Wakitipo on water skis.

S is for School

As my family relocated constantly, I went to many, many schools. My family decided that I functioned better in Catholic schools, as my quiet and introverted nature appreciated the structure and discipline, two things that were not apparent in my family home, unless I was living with my grandmother.

I was schooled in the tail end of the days of Catholic brutality so my memories are punctuated with intense experiences that were both incredibly positive and very negative.

I loved reading and was happiest in the world created by books and my own imagination. I never bonded with other children, although by and large I enjoyed school. I must have been the only person I have ever encountered who had her parents called in by the school to say they were worried about how quiet and unnaturally absorbed by school work I was.

My reports were always superb and that was expected. Initially I had wanted to be an archaeologist, which later morphed to medicine, then law.

I rarely had friends, which may have been because I was always the new arrival or perhaps because I never played or mixed with the other children.

I can't remember being bullied although I have vague recollections of name calling; however that never really bothered me.

At one school I received a pass to use the toilet during class time, and once there proceeded to roll toilet paper rolls along the floor and around the building.

Why? I have no idea.

By the age of eleven I had been to 15 schools, but the constant travelling stopped when my parents separated and my life became more stable.

Unfortunately this stability meant that I drifted from any academic striving which had previously given me so much solace. Until I left school at 16, I gradually and exponentially lost interest in the grind of applied study.

S is for Squats

I made my first trip to London when I was 20. I quickly ran out of money and being unable to pay rent, I started squatting with a group of friends in a disused hotel in Earls Court.

We were a diverse group. Wagner the Brazilian who loved guns; Monika, the Italian who loved cocaine; Robin the Australian whose television had correctly told her the wins and places of the Melbourne cup (when it was switched off). Robin had a paid Tunisian lover called Marco whom we rarely saw. If we did he was invariable wearing sheer briefs and looking impressively muscular and oiled.

There was also a deranged Irishman whose name eludes me. When drunk he would ride motorcycles through the living room, dive through windows and get in violent, nihilistic and doomed fights.

We had just received an eviction notice from our Earl's Court squat. None of us had any idea of where to go.

I was in Fulham Broadway DSS, sorting out my unemployment benefit after I was sacked from my bar job for turning up to work with no shoes on (I had lost one of my only pair of shoes, when drunk). I was sitting on a screwed to the floor aluminium chair waiting to see one of the advisors who was hiding behind reinforced glass.

While watching an old lady start a fire with her paper work in the aisle, I caught the darting eyes of an obvious cocaine user.

He beckoned me outside and we had a joint, a line or two of coke and chatted. I told him about my imminent eviction at which he dredged a huge bunch of keys out from his briefcase (yes, he carried a brief case) and asked where we wanted to live.

I took him back to Earls Court and introduced him to my compatriots.

We then proceeded to move to a building in Sloane Square that had been converted into luxury flats yet to be put on the market.

David, our aforementioned saviour, converted the basement flat of this building into a den for himself, and we occupied the upstairs flats.

A friend of David's would frequently come and visit, sometimes for days at a time, always accompanied by his huge ghetto blaster which I later discovered was used to carry vast quantities of drugs.

I once went downstairs to ask David for something or other. David and his friend pulled me into the flat, maniacally barking nonsense at me whilst proffering a variety of pills, coke, and acid dredged from David's briefcase.

I was locked in that room for three days whilst David raved, took drugs, made toast, threw the still plugged in toaster out the window, played music, threw the live heater out the window and took more drugs.

I took plenty of drugs too. The routine went something like, take some acid then take a downer to calm down the acid, then take some speed and coke to speed things up again, then the acid doesn't seem to work so take more acid. Meanwhile continuously drink and smoke hash. I stopped counting trips I had dropped at six, and from then on I would just pretend to take the acid they were aggressively offering me, until I realised that I had been imprisoned and needed to try and keep relatively clear headed so I could survive this madness.

The others from the building tried to get me out (or tried to get in, I'm still not sure which). Eventually I was released. Ten minutes later, the house was raided. The police arrested David and his friend.

We proved very loyal for such recently acquired friends and went to David's court case in Brixton. I can't remember what the charges were but he was remanded on bail for quite a while.

We were paid to vacate the Sloane Square residence by its owners. By the time we needed to move out David had reappeared with his potent bunch of keys.

We then moved to another empty boarding house in Earls Court. Once more David took over the basement, which he converted into a nightclub.

I was David's 'mirror girl' who is akin to an usher selling ice-creams and sweets in an old fashioned movie house, except my wares were a mirror, inhalation tubes and drugs (speed to the left, coke to the right).

I discovered that our insane saviour had a doctor who would write him scripts for anything. I utilised the knowledge of pharmaceuticals I had acquired in New Zealand, to give David drug shopping lists, which he would obtain for me, free, and with needles.

David's 'office' was equipped with a large desk, behind which he hung an array of underwear belonging to women that he had slept with, and from where he would supervise various debauches.

One day I was woken up by a commotion outside the front door. I went out to see Monika being held by her dreadlocks having her head bashed against railings by a veiled Arabic woman, who was accompanied by her two children and husband.

They were the owners of the building.

We were eventually driven out of this squat in a more violent and less civilised manner than that of Sloane Square. After a brief time sitting on mounds of our possessions on the footpath, we moved into a squat in a housing estate in Fulham Broadway.

I think that David's sentencing must have occurred by then for he disappeared into Brixton Prison. Our numbers rapidly dissipated, as this squat was a nasty, flea ridden one bedroom flat. I was having trouble opening the front door one day, gave it a hard push and it fell off. At that point I knew it was time to leave.

I wrote to my family's doctor in Hong Kong to see if I could borrow the money to leave England. He wrote me a letter saying that I needed a good spanking, but did lend me the money. I can't remember if I actually paid him back....

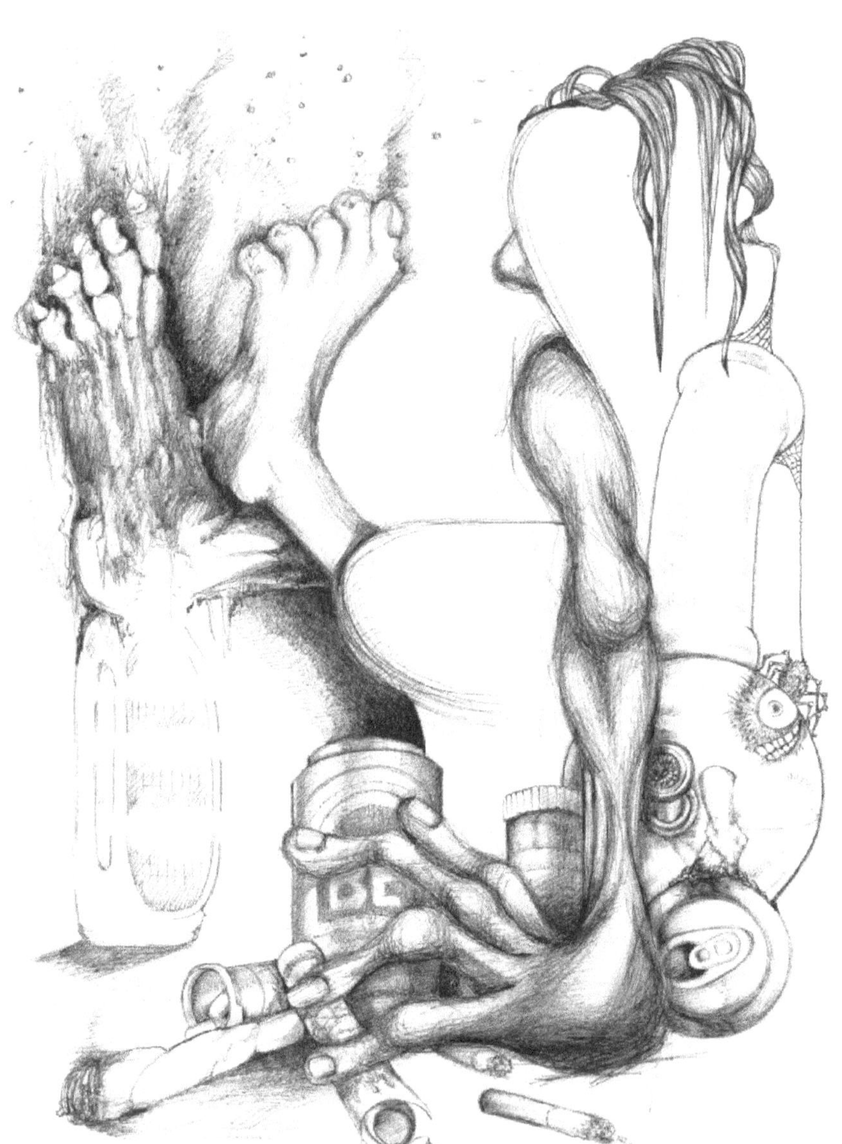

T is for: Terry

T is for Terry

I can't remember when or how I first met Terry. I must have been about 17 and still living in Wellington.

He was a tall, lean, good looking boy about the same age as myself, and very enthusiastic about making money. He had recently set up business as a call boy and waxed lyrical about the two of us starting an escort agency.

We got on exceptionally well and enjoyed the same drugs although our physical relationship never progressed beyond the occasional stoned fumble.

About a year into our friendship I started flatting with him and his sister. Several months later Terry came off his motorbike and broke his back. Terry would spend the rest of his life paralysed from the chest down although he still had movement in his arms.

I keep in touch with him during his times in various hospitals and went to visit him at the spinal unit in Christchurch. This place was oppressive and depressing, filled with young men who had been involved in motorbike accidents lying in hospital beds on their backs, gripped in emotional darkness.

We made a canopy and painted it, so Terry would have something to look at as he laid face upwards. Later for his birthday celebrations we moved his bed outside the ward into the sun.

We arranged live music, drink and drugs in abundance. We all (Terry included) got incredibly stoned. I still remember the horror of wandering around that hospital, lost and tripping.

When Terry came out of hospital he used his compensation money to buy a Jag, a Staffordshire bull terrier, an electric cattle prod, and set himself up in business as a drug dealer.

Although he had no use of his lower limbs, he still drove a manual transmission car by using a stick on the pedals. When he was stoned, these rides were terrifying.

We kept in touch for some years. Drug connections notwithstanding, we retained our fondness for each other although he could be obnoxious, difficult and pugnacious.

His paralysis combined with his addiction created many problems for him; some minor albeit unpleasant such as untended and pungent colostomy bags and catheters, others more serious such as nodding off when stoned and setting fire to his feet which were too close to an electric fire. As he couldn't feel anything he didn't notice until the smell of burning flesh became overpowering.

Terry was another bright spark and huge personality that I lost contact with. I don't know whether he survived or not.

T is for Things (of the Spirit)

Whilst I was too sturdy to be considered 'fey' I always had a strong fascination for the mysterious, the arcane and the occult. When I grew older it wasn't so odd a thing, especially in the drug-using world, but as a child this interest caused a little anxiety in my parents. It would have created great friction if my extremely Catholic grandmother had cottoned onto my leanings. However I was shrewd enough when I lived with her, to hide in books of fairytales and archaeological tomes which were less likely to offend or cause her to call in the exorcist or local priest for a 'chat'.

I was given book vouchers as Christmas and birthday presents. When I turned seven I used these to buy a subscription of *Man Myth and Magick*. One of the magazines had a series of photographs of naked covens that sent my father into a paroxysm of puritanical rage. I was forced to return the subscription but instead came back with a book on *Witchcraft and Demonology* that somehow slipped through the family censorship net.

As my father was an atheist and my mother indifferent there wasn't much emphasis on the spiritual when I was a child, unless I was living with my grandmother who was a fundamentalist Roman Catholic.

All my schools were also rigorously Catholic, but somehow none of this touched me. Whilst I found the glamour of the Roman Catholic religion and rituals fascinating, they never moved me nor affected my innermost views on the nature of reality.

By my early teens I had mastered palmistry and tarot reading and had a voracious appetite for magically orientated spiritually, whatever tradition it stemmed from, as well as a strong aversion to hierarchical and structured religions.

Religious Studies was a favourite subject at school, which I did at examination level and in my brief foray into academe I studied the phenomenology of religion.

I realise that my spiritual obsessions were a creative way of imposing order in my own chaotic world, it worked for me. It gave me a sense of power or rightness which I never lost, although in my last year of addiction I became very disconnected from this inner spiritual strength.

I practised meditation, learned yoga, experimented with trance and psychedelics. I occasionally discussed with therapists my interests and beliefs whilst steering them away from questions as to whether the television and radio ever had specific messages directed towards me.

In my 20s a wealthy Indian girlfriend of mine became involved with a cultish type group in Hong Kong. She knew my interests in belief systems so she asked me to come with her to check them out.

This group was based in the New Territories, which was then a relatively isolated area. It was run by a western woman who claimed that she was an incarnation of Christ, although the group she formed had a very Eastern structure with various robed Indian priests wandering around. I clashed with the leader, who tried to undermine my confidence (as debating theological points with me got her nowhere). Whilst the group was obviously bogus, I still found the meetings very upsetting; their tactics were obviously a psychological undermining of my self esteem.

I was assigned an Indian teacher with whom I was supposed to be able to discuss the group's teachings. He was removed from his mentoring role when he revealed he had lascivious thoughts towards me. I never bothered returning to the enclave.

Treatment centres, although not allied to any particular religion, still very actively discouraged me from pursuit of my own spiritual predilections taking away my tarot deck and various books. After leaving these facilities I spent some time exploring the new age movement, trance and dance groups and things of a similar ilk which I found interesting but not right for me.

It wasn't until I made a conscious decision to start exploring my darker more 'woo woo' side that I felt myself again; there seems to be a parallel between my own spirituality, my creative expression and a basic animism that works and IS me.

I went through periods over the years of reading palms or cards for basic remuneration or cigarettes, but although I was apparently very good, I always felt uncomfortable doing it.

I qualified in and practiced alternative therapies and later did basic spell craft for people. Never having been the best at relating intimately with others, I found this to be incredibly stressful. Again I was good at doing what was needed and had enough insight gained from my rather chequered life experiences to stand me in good stead on the more practical aspects of dealing with people on this level. This type of work, however, fostered needy, unhealthy, dependant relationships which I had trouble coping with, so I stepped well back from it and have been much happier for that.

T is for (The) Troubles

After several years I forgot how miserable I had been in my first attempt to live in London, so I returned. This time I tried to do it differently, armed with references, a CV, savings and lists of people to see who might help me establish myself in a well paid respectable career.

Within a week I ran into an old friend living in Brixton and scuppered my opiate free existence by having a hit of heroin.

Within two weeks I had a pub job, and a several weeks after that I was sleeping with the bar's manager. Lack of money meant I moved out of my new flat and was soon living with him above the pub.

The Duke of Edinburgh in central Brixton was run down and basic having had various incarnations as a front for drug dealing and before that prostitution, with no renovations in between.

There were rats in the cellar, the beer lines were filthy; the whole place was generally a health risk and safety hazard.

The man I moved in with was an Irishman called Paedar. He was morbidly obese, intensely patriotic and loyal to Ireland to the point of fanaticism.

Despite claiming to have long term experience in pub management he seemed to have no idea of how to run a public house. The Duke of Edinburgh's clientele were predominantly Jamaican. There was the older generation that played dominoes with vigour, worked exceptionally hard in generally low paid jobs, and strangely enough many of them voted for Margaret Thatcher. Then there were the younger generation many of whom opted for a more street type existence. There was some sort of bond between the Irish and the Jamaicans; a general feeling of being outcast or abused by British society.

I remember one old man quoting to me - 'the Irish built the roads, the Jamaicans swept them, and the English walk on them'.

After some lock-ins when everyone was heavily drunk, 'Molly Malone' would come on the juke box and the Jamaican/Irish clientele would erupt in singing 'cockles and mussels' - an incongruous experience.

I never could figure out why Paedar ended up in Brixton. He had no experience of running a pub, although he was skilled at working behind a bar and played a superb game of snooker. I assumed he was there for money laundering or some such thing.

Every weekend he would get visitors over from Ireland. Large Irishmen in suits both called John Joe, one with an impressive dent in his forehead, who were charming but hard as nails.

When we had these visits, Paedar and I would go with them on their rounds of various other Irish pubs to see people, generally in Shepherds Bush but occasionally in Bermondsey.

Paedar once said to me that the pubs we went to were all IRA, that they owned the fruit machines, which yielded a large income.

However I was never sure with him what was truth, what was a lie, so I stayed in my own little world. This insular world was gradually becoming smaller but kept from contracting completely by my continuing connection to my friend Jill and the occasional use of heroin.

My relationship with Paedar quickly became subtly abusive. He was exceptionally jealous and possessive, and didn't like me to go out without him. He was sure that like most women, I was constantly looking for another man.

He regarded libraries, parks, and churches as all places where women went to 'pull men'. Eye contact was forbidden; clothes were censored if they were considered to be too provocative. He withheld my wages as part of this control. Strangely I let all this happen.

I didn't love him; found him physically unattractive (our sex life was very pedestrian as he was so overweight, most sexual positions were limited). Although intelligent he didn't read and had no interest in anything other than sports, snooker, alcohol and everything Irish.

At one point an Irish friend of his, Ollie, moved into the pub before going back to Ireland. Police had found Semtex in his flat.

This was a time in London when there were a lot of IRA bombings. If the trains on the underground stalled for longer than a few minutes, commuters would start to get very uneasy. Anti Irish sentiment was high and the community I mixed with definitely closed ranks.

However I was detached from all of this, I simply didn't think about all of these strange activities or comings and goings.

One night Paedar took me to see a *Wolftones* concert in Clapham which was an amazing and surreal experience.

I'd heard the music before (the *Wolftones* and rebel music was favoured by the Jamaican clientele of the Duke of Edinburgh at the late night lock-ins) but wasn't prepared for the live experience.

The security guards used metal detectors at the entrance to make sure no one had weapons. Inside the venue it was a cross between a free Ireland march and a football match with people waving flags, pints of Guinness and general bedlam all around. I think this concert must have been the only time I went out with Paedar to somewhere that wasn't a pub.

Soon after Ollie left we moved to another pub in Dulwich. This one was more of an Irish workingmen's bar. Like the Duke of Edinburgh, The Castle was also run very down although that didn't affect the enormous takings. The customers, predominantly builders, could come in post work in their dirt-crusted boots without fear of messing up a carpet, knock back ten pints then go home. This part of Dulwich had an Irish vigilante group who kept the area crime free without involving the police.

Paedar cleared out the safe after a Saturday night heavy drinking session and caught the plane back to Ireland; without my knowing, of course.

Thus I lost my partner, my job and my home. It was time to move onto the next phase in my life.

U is for Underdog

I hitchhiked to Dunedin from Wellington to go to a party and had been waylaid by a drinking session in a friend's house-truck.

I passed out and when I came to, everyone had left, so I found a phone booth and rang the contact number I had for the address of the gathering. A woman answered with an obvious party in full swing around her. She was extremely drunk, but she chatted a little with me then gave me directions.

This woman was Hazel, someone who was destined to become one of my life's most abiding and longest running friendships.

Hazel's mother was schizophrenic and had abandoned Hazel and her brother before being sectioned to an institution for the rest of her life. Hazel was three and her brother younger when they were discovered, living on food scraps from rubbish bins.

They were separated and Hazel spent the following years in institutions and foster homes where she was horrifically physically and sexually abused. When she was sixteen she was raped and beaten by several men while hitchhiking, then had her legs broken.

When I met her she had the look of a punk rocker with a lot of the attitude. Her fine red hair was cropped with a long fringe; she wore tights, Doctor Martins and black vests. Hazel wasn't a pretty woman, quite the opposite. She also had moments of madness and rage. She was a punk poet, but under all the aggression, had a softness that was revealed in her art.

Why we bonded so much and so strongly I'll never really know. Hazel believed that we were soul sisters, to which I am inclined to agree.

People around us used to comment on our relationship as superficially we were so different, but at heart we both shared a love of mysticism and believed in magick and fairy tales.

I lived with her when I had messed up at whatever place I was staying. She always looked after me; sometimes she would actually physically attack those that she felt were hurting or abusing me.

I didn't have many female friends partially due to my perceived behaviour around men, partially because I was emotionally very inaccessible, and partially because my priority in life was getting wasted and there were few women who lived like that and were not in insular relationships. The drug using world tends to be male dominated.

Hazel loved me unconditionally and wanted nothing from me except friendship which was a great and valued thing for me at that time.

I did have a few male friends but there was often an underlying sexual tension. It wasn't unusual for me to come to after a drunken sleep to find one of these men having sex with me. I wondered for a long time what pleasure there could be in having sex with someone unconscious but realised it wasn't necessarily about pleasure, but possession.

Hazel's fridge had heavy chains and a padlock, as she never recovered from a fear of being hungry or abandoned.

She had three cats, all ginger, all female (which is rare with ginger cats as they are generally male). I remember us going away for five days; she laid out five bowls of food for them, in a row, one for each day.

Like me Hazel was a heavy drinker although she wasn't interested in drugs apart from the occasional mushroom trip. She loved Katavit, the liquid speed that was given to the elderly, which made her very mellow.

When I was living with Martyn, Hazel came around with Peter, a man that she had met in a pub. He had a job, seemed quite straight although was obviously entranced by her.

She was drunk which made her rude and abusive towards him. I took her aside and said to her that perhaps this man would love her unconditionally and look after her, that she should give him a chance and stick with him.

Over 20 years later they are still together. Hazel is very ill and unable to have much contact with anyone anymore, even via computer, but I'll never forget her.

V is for Violin

I was 20 and living in Melbourne after some time in Hong Kong and London. I loved Melbourne and still regard it as my favourite place to live. I was working in a legal brothel that paid exceptionally well.

My flatmate was also a New Zealander. One night a friend of hers, who had moved over from Dunedin in New Zealand came to visit. I opened the door for Sean; it was boom bang, instant love on both sides.

That night we talked excitedly, falling further and deeper into a passionate, obsessive love. We partied hard, drinking heavily and taking his pills (sedatives to control his bipolar disorder). I had come off the opiate habit I had acquired in London so was consuming with more than usual gusto.

Sean and I would lie in bed watching past lives drift past in which we had taken turns to destroy the other; the last one being when he had been a landowner, whilst I was white trash who worked on his farmland. He had raped and strangled me, then afterwards thrown my body in a ditch.

All pretty out there in some respects but very powerful, very real at the time. Overwhelmingly so ... I even had visions of the position on a map where this life had supposedly occurred.

Creatively it was also immense. We wrote, drew, and grew thin with passionate excitement.

We decided to move back to Dunedin to get married, Sean returning first to house hunt. He found a room in an old convent with oak panelling, high ceilings and strange passageways. When I moved in all was initially wonderful, however things changed when I started to reconnect with my old friends (creative junkie types) and he with his (creative pretentious types).

Sean was a near legend on the Flying Nun (a seminal and legendary New Zealand record label) music and art scene, whereas my fame was of a more notorious sort that lay in my beauty, my ability to consume mood altering substances, party hard and sleep with near everyone.

One night Sean took me to the top floor of the building which had originally been the nun's dormitory.

There was a full moon shining through a large circular window which took up the entire end wall. Sean played the violin to me, and then taught me to waltz. I felt as if all the spirits past of the nuns looked on, sighing with the beauty of it all.

Later when we moved into a 1920s house, things became more strained. I was not at all domestic, just wanting to party whilst Sean wanted to suffer and live a quiet and artistic life. We both grew thinner then Sean became physically ill.

We fought a lot, as my morality was very different to his. He was perpetually anxious that I would return to prostitution.

He went away for a few days on some music business in Christchurch and I had a group of friends around. We had a session on the 'old moot', a local apple wine notorious for its stupor inducing black outs.

Sean came back to find our little group, naked, tangled up and unconscious on and in his bed.

In the final days of our relationship, he was in bed ill so I went out for healing supplies but became waylaid. I returned three days later with an astronomical telescope for him, which he was too angry to appreciate.

We drifted further apart. Sean's illness and mania increased until he was admitted to hospital with glandular fever.

He rang me from his hospital bed saying, I still remember these words so well, 'that he was spitting out hunks of his tonsils that looked like desiccated mince and that talking to me just made him feel worse'. Then he went on to say that I destroyed everything and was destroying him and that he wanted me to move out and have nothing more to do with him.

This I did, although I was devastated. I still loved him very, very much.

I went on a pilgrimage of sorts to Wellington, then hitchhiked my way back to Dunedin where I continued on a bender of massive proportions until Martyn, another musician, managed to supply me with opiates to keep me away from drinking. Once I had a habit, Martyn became my partner and then husband.

V is for Virginity

I have absolutely no idea when I lost my virginity. When I was in my early teens, I was very much a girl whom boys had sexual encounters with rather than relationships; so it is possible that one of these lads, in a drunk and aggressive manner, finger fucked my virginity away.

Later I didn't seem to have a mental line that differentiated between a kiss and sex, so I would have sex with near anyone who wanted to. Ironically if I cared about someone, I tended to hold out a little longer.

There was a point in my late teens when men I knew who were troubled with a residual virginity, would ask to have sex with me. Generally I found this was a pretty lack lustre experience as young men may have stamina but not much in the way of technique, although there was one example where all the usual rules were overturned and the man in question was a natural hedonist and proved to be incredible in bed.

I think that my behaviour and the ease with which I drifted into prostitution were considered symptomatic of someone who had been sexually abused, although later it was also very much the morality of the drug culture. Within that sphere of society, sex wasn't as important as drugs, and homosexuality or bisexuality wasn't considered, you simply had sex with whoever was around regardless of gender.

Saying that, sexual activity was very dependent on the drugs you were taking. Sex on opiates were prolonged affairs where ejaculation often wasn't an option and you would constantly be nodding off mid act and wake up with your face between your partner's legs, after having a brief, drugged nap. Sex whilst drunk tended to be more of an indiscriminate debauch, where anything was acceptable and blackouts eased any guilt or shame.

In one flat I was living in I was woken early in the morning by hysterical yelling. A drunken friend had climbed into what he thought was a woman's bed and started trying to have sex with her, but it turned out it was her five year old son that he was trying to romance. The child was unharmed and seemed rather bemused at the furore his temporary bed partner had created.

That particular gentleman was then in the early stages of 'wet brain' and later cut his own throat.

I have talked to lovers I had in my early to late teens and they said that having sex with me was rather one sided, with me being a very passive participant. Later I became much more enthusiastic when I moved beyond the dislocation of body and emotions, and fear of losing control that eating disorders and drugs produced.

When I stopped using drugs and slept with someone for the first time without any chemicals or alcohol in my system, I was thirty years old. I imagine it would have been very similar to losing one's virginity. I was self conscious, clumsy and very nervous.

My partner who was also in early recovery from drug addiction afterwards shared at an Narcotics Anonymous meeting about our first fuck, saying that I had no idea how to put a condom on. It dispelled any hopes for him that I may have picked up some erotic tricks in my years of working in the sex industry.

Some years ago I was re reading J M Barrie's *Peter Pan.* In the beginning there is mention of Mrs Darling, Wendy's mother, having a kiss tucked in the corner of her mouth. No matter how hard Mr Darling tried he could never get that kiss, and she eventually gave it to Peter Pan.

For some of us, virginity is like that 'private kiss'; it is something beyond a physical act that can never be taken, only given. The thing is many of us never get a chance to realise this.

V is for Voices

In my 20s I was working in a pub in Herne Hill and living a double life of sorts. As my income was low I only used heroin a few times a week so was either withdrawing or stoned.

Initially I had been living in a flat so my finances were even more strained, but when I started living in the pub I was working in, then went on a methadone programme, I had much more financial freedom.

I started a relationship with the pub's trainee manager who had no idea about my drug use. I had visits from various suspect friends who would surreptitiously slide a matchbox across the bar for me to retrieve and then scuttle to the nearest toilet and consume. My work mates seemed to have no clue about my alternate life.

At one stage I was asked on a date with a very good looking pub regular, however any potential romance was destroyed when the weed and drink which he produced proved to be dynamite when combined with my maintenance dose of methadone, and I started to hallucinate.

Another time, on a sunny day, I went across the road to meet a friend and score. In full view of my boss and boyfriend (who were sitting on the benches outside the bar) a police van pulled myself and my dealer over, took us into the back of the van and stripped searched us.

Luckily I had swallowed my glad-wrapped portion of smack (which I later threw up and injected) but even now I am impressed at how I managed to lie my way out of that, just as I lied my way around my bruised swollen hands, constant covering of my scarred arms, lack of money and need to go daily to the chemist and weekly to Maudsley Hospital.

Pubs in the UK then were very much a social centre. Daily customers with their regular drinks invariably became friendly with bar staff.

Donald was an older man who with his heavy belly, protruding lower lip, constant dry sometimes frothing mouth, who was obviously on medication for some form of mental illness. I used to chat with him, as he was bright, quirky, well read and interesting.

Donald developed a crush of sorts on me. Over time I found out that he used to work with the British Museum's rare books and manuscripts until voices told him that he was dealing with the words of the devil. He started to destroy some of these literary treasures, at which point he was removed from his position and pensioned off.

Donald was invited to a preview of an exhibition of the work of William Blake at the Museum, and asked me to accompany him. The poor man was very nervous as this was an exclusive and prestigious event, all red carpet, celebrity art critics and silken ropes.

As we approached the Museum his moribund and drugged bladder couldn't cope with the strain. He had to relieve himself by the Museum main steps.

Anyway, it was a nice evening.

I'm not sure what happened to him, although I had a dim recollection that he was found in dead in an apartment piled high with paper and books.

W is for: Wanchai

W is for Wanchai

As I was a difficult teenager in an institution, I didn't accompany my family to Hong Kong when they relocated there.

However my stepfather's ex pat terms meant that his company paid for yearly trips for me to visit.

Hong Kong was an incredible place, far more than the proverbial world away from the fetid drug addled squats and house trucks I lived in at that time in New Zealand.

Initially my family lived in the mid levels in Hong Kong, a place that still had surviving remnants of an older Asian culture.

There was Central Market, where all types of endangered creatures could be found living, trussed and hanging or in buckets of water; Ladder Street with its traditional tailors who could copy haute couture clothing perfectly in 24 hours; an old castle on Mid Levels; cages on Kowloon side which the homeless locked themselves and their possessions into at night; a black leopard in a tiny cage on Mid Level's at which small children aimed water pistols and slingshots; and everywhere hoards of people moving at an accelerated pace.

There were beggars in every shape and form; opium addicts crusted within dirty rags and dreadlocks; people with no limbs or limbs that were fused to them after explosions of the highly inflammable chemicals in sweatshops they worked in.

There were also the incredibly rich, some incongruous in their work as street vendors or owners of market stalls.

My mother was a member of The Foreign Correspondent Club, an old style bastion of print and photo-journalism. The walls of the club were lined with images of luminaries such as Larry Burroughs; waiters remembered your name, membership number and favoured drink; the bar was propped up by some of the most interesting and well lived (and worn) people I have ever got completely smashed with.

I was at the bar when the live news feed showed a reporter and photographer (Bill Latch and Neil Davis) being shot in an attempted coup in Bangkok in 1985. The cameraman dropped his camera as he was killed and it carried on filming after it hit the ground. The bar went silent as people watched their compatriots dying and these tough foreign correspondents that had seen so much, wept.

The more upmarket nightclub area was Lan Kwai Fong, very expensive and open to occasional celebrity spotting (if you cared which I didn't). I would party with the rich and famous in clothes borrowed from my mother. I'd snort cocaine in nightclub toilets, fall into rubbish bins which I'd have to be helped out of, and stagger home past 1000s of rats scampering in formation around closed restaurant fronts, and the washing being hung out in the prison across from the Foreign Correspondent Club.

Sometimes I would go straight from a bar to breakfast at a local congee (a sort of rice gruel) place where at five in the morning workman would be breakfasting, birdcages with tiny birds in them on the tables.

The chemists in Hong Kong sold pretty much anything, including very strong painkillers and diet pills, which in most countries were prescription only, so I was well catered for.

We used to take the ferry over to Macau for shopping trips to buy my mother's medication (benzo-diazapams mainly). I would invariably buy a few extras for myself, as the synthetic opiates which I wasn't able to buy in Hong Kong, were available there.

My favourite place to party though was Wanchai. This was less socially constrained and more traditional than Lan Kwai Fong without delving into the realms of the obviously Triad run and very dangerous areas in Kowloon, where every now and then there would be a case of someone running amok with a chopper or a Westerner going missing and being found floating in the harbour.

There were bars such as 'Pussycats' and 'Neptune's', which were pick-up bars for the local prostitutes and their potential customers or the foreign domestic helpers who hoped to meet a husband as an alternative to a life as a maid. However I just wanted to party and was no threat to them nor they to me.

There was an odd little bar called 'Hot Lips', which was full of old ladies in traditional pyjamas, grey hair in buns, knitting. These were woman who made their fortunes as prostitutes during the Korean and Vietnam War, often investing their earnings shrewdly, and educating their children in private and exclusive American or British schools and universities. Occasionally older men would visit on a nostalgic trip to the Asia they had first encountered during the war and wanted to meet up with a woman they had met at this time.

I was in Wanchai during the first Gulf War and it was utter madness. The American servicemen had been months on their ships in the Gulf without leave so they hit the bars of Hong Kong with a vengeance, pumping millions into the economy daily.

The British forces that were permanently stationed there were not given leave to go into Central Hong Kong during this time for fear of fighting. The number of MPs on duty were cranked up to the nth degree.

Aside from the fact that the American servicemen had not had any R&R for months, they believed that they were going to die when they returned to the Gulf. Many of them had their families flown to Hong Kong to spend time with them, so there was a frantic air to their socialising.

I would go to Wanchai on my usual drinking sprees and see a choreographed bedlam the likes of which I have never seen before. On one side of the street would be the bar girls looking resplendent, on the other side of the street 100s of servicemen. A look, a nod and boom bang, connection made.

Men were being carried out of bars, the dancing and drinking was bacchalian; however there was no fighting or conflict.

Rampant socialising and alcohol consumption aside, I did work during my time in Hong Kong, especially when I started to spend longer periods there as my innate inability to make life work for me in New Zealand, became apparent. At one stage I was a cadet journalist at the South China Morning Post, which was an absolute failure. I wanted to write and enjoyed the different approach to using language, but I didn't have the assertive personality necessary to be a good journalist.

My mentor was an Australian sports journalist; a lovely man and great teacher although his aggressive lustiness (despite being married and having only recently recovered from cancer) was something I couldn't cope with, it just added to my reasons for not staying the course with this particular career.

I was also a beauty therapist, which seemed to be very much an in occupation for young women trying to recover from substance abuse problems in Hong Kong.

I did voluntary work. Riding for the Disabled was an experience as there were no provisions at that time for the mentally and physically infirm, who were thought to bring shame on the family. Deng Xiaoping eventually came out about having a disabled child which brought with it a sea change of attitude, but before that disabled children were farmed out to brutal institutions and some were killed at birth or hidden away. One man had been kept in a cupboard on a junk since early childhood. His muscles had atrophied from being in such an enclosed space, so we stretched and massaged his twisted limbs every day.

I later helped out at a closed camp for Vietnamese Refugees (this was just before their forced repatriation). The camp was within a traditional prison, moated, with barbed wire around it. The Japanese had used it during their occupation of Hong Kong to hold non military POWs.

This was a depressing place. These refugees had predominantly been fishermen and farmers who lived a very physical existence. The area they were imprisoned in didn't have enough space to play even a game of football. Some had been there for seven years; it was truly tragic the way they would question me about New Zealand, a place they gave a near Utopian status.

On my first day there we had some donated toys for the children. If I remember rightly it was dolls for the girls, plastic dinosaurs for the boys. There were enough toys to distribute to every child under seven but Asian children are notoriously difficult to determine the age of.

These people had near no possessions, a riot broke out as people crowded around us, thrusting their children forward, clamouring to receive one of these treasured items. I and the other volunteers ended up barricaded in the office until help arrived.

I was supposed to have been teaching English, although really I coached my pupils how to fill out basic processing forms. My first class was interrupted by security guards coming in to take two of my pupils for suspected plague. Conditions on the boats were so horrendous they encouraged diseases such as plague, cholera and typhoid.

With Thatcher providing no hoped for succour and the approach of 1997, there was a panic to obtain UK passports and a possible safe haven from the Chinese Regime. Tiananmen Square fuelled this panic further. I jumped into the melee of the panic stricken and obtained my British passport. As I had a British Passport, I used to extend my visa to stay by making trips to Macau and getting a new visa each time I returned to Hong Kong.

I loved Hong Kong. I loved the contrasts of old Chinese architecture and gleaming skyscrapers, the pomposity of the ex pats, the energy of the entrepreneur, the stories that were told and the history being created.

In what other place could you go out after work and in the long, hard drinking evening that followed, have a conversation with a journalist who had covered the Vietnam war; be taught how to dance 'southern style' by an American serviceman; run into the family doctor who prescribes your opiate antagonists in a transsexual bar at four in the morning; see in the sunrise in a local market cafe where the coffee is mixed with sweetened condensed milk and brewed in a vat, and there are 100s of beautiful birds in bamboo cages on the tables, singing in the dawn.

It was a hard and in many ways superficial place, but Gods I lived life fully there.

W is for Warrior

Henry was one of the few in my social circle who worked in a mainstream job. He had a picture framing business which he tried to teach me the basics of, but I never got very far with due to more pressing concerns orientated around inebriation.

At one time Henry needed to deliver goods to various parts of the South Island of New Zealand so he agreed to take a few others and me with him for company whilst driving.

We stopped in Christchurch and were sitting in the square in the centre of the city, outside the cathedral, watching life and the tourists when a group of people came up to us that several of our number knew.

One of these people was Robert and he was pure kinetic energy. He was an archetypical warrior; very lean, always striving to go forth and adventure. In the eyes of mainstream society Robert was considered to be schizophrenic although at that point he wasn't on medication.

Robert joined us for the remainder of our journey, which needless to say was chaotic and at times dangerous. At one point we were visiting some friends of friends in an isolated anarchist's compound on the West Coast.

They were stockpiling weapons for a 'day of reckoning', and learning self-sufficiency whilst consuming huge amounts of mushrooms.

They all had sideways X tattooed on their foreheads, which didn't create much peace of mind in us.

We stayed a night (a harrowing experience to say the least) and when we tried to leave the next morning Henry's van wouldn't start. It turns out a part had 'gone missing' from the engine but one of our number managed to cobble a substitute together and we drove out of there very, very relieved.

Some years later I heard rumours that this group had experimented with cannibalism, and whilst this may well have simply been rumour, my experience of that group was that they were more than capable of doing this.

After our adventures with Henry in his magic van I continued to hear about Robert from various people who had knew him. He had always lived in fear of ending up like his father, a schizophrenic who had kidnapped someone, creating a siege and hostage scenario for a week or so in the 1970s, until the police had caught him. He was committed for life in an asylum, where he was medicated to obese incapacity.

After many years Robert's father escaped which generated a media frenzy and general public panic. He was found 24 hours later, dead from hypothermia, at the edge of the grounds of the asylum he had been incarcerated in. He had spent so many years weak and immobilised from his medication that when he fled, he simply fell over and wasn't able to get up again.

This fear of becoming like his notorious parent fuelled Robert's own madness. When his flatmates found him getting more and more erratic in behaviour to the point they became frightened, which is saying something, as they were a tough group.

When his housemate Donna woke up one morning with Robert sitting by her bed with a baseball bat muttering to himself, she contacted a mental health unit and Robert was forcibly put on monthly injections.

At one point he stopped turning up for these shots as he couldn't cope with the thought of turning into a slow and jelly like blob. Robert was tracked down, caught and like his father, sectioned.

The last I heard he was in the same asylum that his father had been in.

W is for Waterbed

I was living in an area of Wellington Aro Street, which constituted a town unto itself, and was inhabited by old hippies, artisans and fringe dwellers.

Across the road from my flat lived a woman in her 40s named Heidi who was close to my friend, Jane. Now Heidi was a prostitute of the old school variety with tattoos, a pugilist's demeanour and attitude.

This was unlike many of my own friends who were working girls, were middle class, educated, and fucked up with habits to feed. Apparently Heidi's ancestors came from Pitcairn Island and she was a descendant of Fletcher Christian.

Heidi had a waterbed, the height of red light consumer glamour in those days. I knew of another prostitute who had also purchased one and had a huge party to celebrate the fact. Jane and I used to look after her house when she was away, and revel on it.

I had decided to move to Dunedin as I had committed a sexual indiscretion, which meant the Aro Street clique community had effectively turned against me en masse. Jane decided to join me on the journey for a visit if not to live. I booked the very early morning ferry. The said indiscretion meant I had been thrown out of my flat and was going to stay with Jane at Heidi's.

Jane procured some acid for us, which being opportunistic and greedy rather than sensible, we took. We stayed out cavorting till late. When we returned to Heidi's, the front door was locked. Heidi must have returned from her holiday and as was her wont, locked us out when she felt that we might return at an inappropriate hour.

Now Heidi was not the sort of woman one woke up, so we went to the spare bedroom in the shed out the back, which was exceptionally cold. Heidi's cat seems to have had explosive diarrhoea over our bed, which added to our misery. We both had a very long, very bad trip until we departed from Wellington at five the next morning.

W is for Weanal (on Fire)

After a particularly hectic night partying, I was woken early the next morning by a roar and a flash of light moving past my partially open bedroom door.

I got out of bed to see my flatmate, Weanal, running up and down the corridor, on fire. He had passed out with candles still burning in his room, and they had set fire to the wall hangings.

I put him out with some towels, sorted out the burning flag in his bedroom, and went back to bed.

I had more than a few friends die in this way.

X is for Xanadu

I read once that before Coleridge finished Kubla Khan, he was interrupted by 'the person from Porlock', a debt collector knocking on his door, and was never able to return to that particular stream of consciousness.

I feel as if I too had a debt collector knocking on the door of my life, breaking and permanently redirecting my concentration.

All life's blessings and gifts were laid out for me to use at will; but the madness that had been building in the chaotic years prior came taptaptapping at my door sometime in my teens, I lost my direction and awareness of where I was for many, many years.

Y is for: Yangzhou

Y is for Yangzhou

When I first went to China, it had just opened up to foreign travel and a Westerner still drew stares. It was a great adventure in those days; so much so I went several times. I saw a man battling with a soldier at the antiquated X-ray machine at the airport when they tried to take away the machine gun that he wanted as carry-on luggage; stayed in hostels in Beijing that were packed full of Russians who had come there to buy basic household supplies; ate dog kebabs (by accident) and saw an execution on a market day in a small township area where the photos of the criminals were afterwards pinned on the village notice board.

I loved the place. It moved and lifted me despite aspects of the country that were terribly cruel and seemingly heartless.

Guangzhou train station was crowded with immigrants who had moved to that area as its status at that time as an economic free zone meant there was a chance to make a fortune, to rise beyond the level of living dictated for the rest of China. Here you would see beggars and addiction but in the rest of China there was a more mainstream poverty, also an almost Mad Max element with its strange vehicles made of what looked to be lawn mower engines and bike handlebars held together with oversized rubber bands.

I was in Beijing when the first MacDonald's opened. The queue went all the way around Tiananmen Square despite the rather limited range of products on offer (fries and coca cola, and perhaps thick shakes).

My favourite place to visit was a small town called Yangzhou just outside Guilin.

An incredibly beautiful place, surrounded by strange shaped mountains that were dripping with foliage; it had only recently been placed on the hippy trail. A few enterprising individuals who had converted rooms into hostels, were selling pancakes and muesli whilst playing the *Pixies* or *Van Morrison* tapes that some intrepid travellers had left behind.

The local people had managed to scrape together local treasures to sell, which I didn't have the money or foresight to purchase but must be worth a fortune now, but hey, I have some amazing memories.

I drank snake wine and local beer with a French pathologist who worked for Citroen sourcing fresh, unclaimed cadavers to use as crash test dummies. That was before he burned out and went travelling. I had a brief drunken affair with him, but given his mental state at that time I suspect he could still be there.

I defecated in concrete huts; where you would look down to see pigs receiving your offerings.

I saw a full moon shining through the mountain of the moon, dumped my bulimia in the Yangzi River never to take it back and saw Cormorant fishing in the most beautiful and serene surrounds.

I see this place in film sets sometimes and it always fills me with joy and excitement. Despite rumours that it has been converted into a theme park, I am determined to return one day.

Z is for Zenith (ending on a high note)

Now I wouldn't go as far as to say this little tome has a happy ending. Those of us, who think too much, feel too deeply or need to express themselves as either a constant or as a flux, are never going to find life to be an easy journey.

However things did eventually even out for me. There is no arguing that combinations of hormones and a rather chaotic childhood meant my early years were an adventure on a good day, a tragedy on most.

I have been privileged to have an innate luck in the way life kept presenting me opportunities to try again and giving me the ingredients to do this.

Eventually I was able to work out how to live this life without the pain, drama and danger; although it took a long time and a lot of help.

So many things have fallen away from me, in many ways this book is a way of laying what was lost to rest. Acknowledging the heroes and the villains, the humour and the sorrow and then turning back to where I am now; assured that I have lived my life fully.

In Memory of Andrew, Andy, Ross, Peter, Lindsey, Shonnie, Anne Marie, Zane, Myra, Geoff,Steve, Lorna, John Holman, John O'Brien, Paul O'Brien, Pockets, Tim, Sam, Jimmy, Mark, Bruce, Johnno and all the raucous children who never grew old

.

OTHER MANDRAKE TITLES

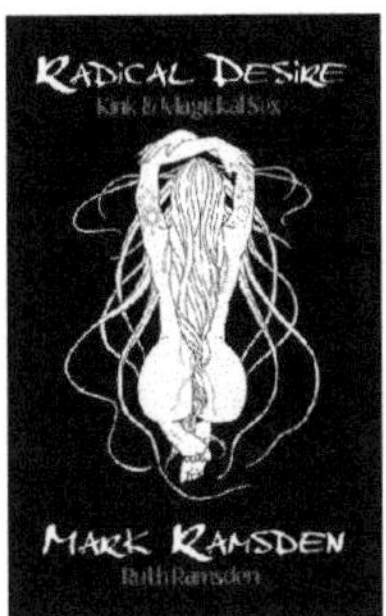

Radical Desire: Kink & Magickal Sex
ISBN 978-1-906958-19-0
£9.99/$14.00

"The wit and wisdom of Mark Ramsden's illuminating text delivers a gripping journey through a rich seam of sexual expression. Read this book, enjoy this book, for it deserves your utmost attention. Over 40? Fat? The style gurus say you're not sexy, not horny, this book says 'Bollocks!' An essential reference work... And bloody good fun too." John Carter

A Contemporary Western Book Of The Dead
Charlotte Rodgers and Lydia Maskell
ISBN 978-1-906958-04-6, £10.99/$14.99

Within this book are rituals, stories, traditions and experiences of magicians' scholars and artists who work with death. Some of the contributors such as Nema, Mogg Morgan, Louis Martine and Nevill Drury (to name but a few) have helped define contemporary transformative spirituality. Others are less well known but just as learned. As there should be in such a collection there is comedy, anger confrontation and practicality.

The Bloody Sacrifice: A personal experience of comtemporary blood rites By Charlotte Rodgers
ISBN 978-1-906958-30-5, £10.99/$20, 155pages

It chronicles her use of road kill and blood in art, ritualised scarification and tattoo work, and the use of venous and menstrual blood in magick. Also included are Charlotte's interviews with tattoo artists; priests from belief systems which utilise blood sacrifice; artists who use their own HIV positive blood as a medium; and those who use mortifications and body modification to effect changes in consciousness and self.

mandrake.uk.net

www.ingramcontent.com/pod-product-compliance
Ingram Content Group UK Ltd.
Pitfield, Milton Keynes, MK11 3LW, UK
UKHW021035060326
468713UK00011B/347